Holt Math
Minnesota
Test Prep Workbook
for Grade 9

HOLT, RINEHART AND WINSTON

A Harcourt Education Company

Orlando • **Austin** • New York • San Diego • London

ISBN-13: 978-0-03-093287-8
ISBN-10:   0-03-093287-4

4 018 08

To the Student

This book is designed to help you practice for the MCA–II in Mathematics. The MCA–II is taken in Grade 11 and measures your proficiency in Math, Reading, and Science.

The book contains practice questions arranged by topic, and practice tests.

The practice questions are organized by content topics. There are 5 topics:

- Number Sense
- Algebra
- Geometry
- Measurement
- Data Analysis, Statistics, and Probability

Within each topic, there are several 2- and 3-page worksheets on each topic. Most questions are multiple choice. Some are gridded response, and others are extended-response.

At the back of the book, the practice tests contain additional practice in each of the strands.

It is a good idea to time yourself as you work some of the practice questions in order to get used to working in a timed situation.

In addition to the practice in this book, your textbook has many opportunities to practice questions in the format of the MCA–II, as well as practice tests and test-taking strategies.

Standardized Test-Taking Strategies for Math

Test Practice
Number Sense

Algebra

Geometry

Measurement

Data Analysis and Probability

v

MCA–II in Brief

Question Format	• Multiple Choice, Gridded Response • Constructed Response
Time Allowed (Mathematics)	4 sessions of approximately 50 minutes per session
Materials Needed	• Number 2 pencils • A 4-function or scientific calculator • Erasers
Links	http://education.state.mn.us/mde/ Accountability_Programs/Assessment_ and_Testing/Assessments/MCA_II/MCA_II_ General_Information/index.html

Standardized Test-Taking Strategies for Math

Standardized tests, such as the MCA–II, are designed in order for you to demonstrate the content and skills you have learned. It is important to keep in mind that, in most cases, the best way to prepare for these tests is to pay close attention in class and take every opportunity to improve your mathematical, reading, and writing skills.

Tips for Taking the Test

Throughout the year

- Keep up with your homework. Homework is important practice that will help you learn the skills you need for the test. Practice will also help you answer questions more quickly, leaving more time for the difficult questions.

- Review your notes, homework, and tests on a regular basis to make sure that you maintain the skills you learned earlier in the year.

- Use flashcards to learn important formulas and vocabulary words. If you can, memorize formulas to save time on the test.

- Familiarize yourself with the format and content of the test.

- Make a timeline for reviewing materials in the time leading up to the test. Do not try to "cram" the night before the test.

- Practice without your calculator, because you will not be allowed to use a calculator on the test.

Before the test

- Be sure you are well rested.

- Eat a good breakfast.

- Be on time, and be sure that you have the necessary materials.

- Be sure to bring any assistive device that you need, such as glasses or a hearing aid.

- Try not to miss class the day before the test. Your teacher may be reviewing important content.

During the Test

- Listen to the instructions of the teacher. It's easy to miss important points that can affect your score.

- Read the directions carefully. If you do not understand a direction, raise your hand and ask for clarification immediately.

- Use your scratch paper. You are more likely to make a mistake when doing a problem in your head. You can also use your written work to help check your answer. Circle the answer and write the problem number next to your work so you can find it while you are reviewing your test.

- Read the entire question, including all answer choices, and think about your answer before you make any marks on the answer sheet.

- Fill in the circle for each answer carefully and completely. Erase any stray marks on the page. If you change an answer choice, be sure to erase completely and carefully so that you do not tear a hole in the answer sheet.

- Make sure the number on the answer document matches the question number in the test booklet.

- Don't spend too much time on any one question. If you cannot answer a question right away, fill in your best choice. If you have time at the end of the test, return to any questions you are unsure of.

- If questions contain negative wording such as NOT, read them carefully and be alert for the use of double negatives within a sentence.

- Understand the format of the test so that you can gauge your time according to what section of the test you are taking.

- If you finish early, review the test and make sure the answer sheet is filled out correctly. Remember, your first answer is usually the correct one, so don't change an answer unless you can convince yourself that your original choice is wrong. Try solving the problem in a different way to see if you get the same answer.

- DON'T STRESS! Just remember what you have learned in class, and you should do well.

Tips for Answering Multiple-Choice Questions

- If there is a figure accompanying the question, review the figure carefully. Read the labels and make sure you understand what the figure represents. Remember, a figure may not be drawn to scale.

- If there is not a figure, it may be helpful to draw one on your scratch paper using the information provided.

- Read the multiple-choice question first for its general intent and then reread it carefully, looking for words that give clues or can limit possible answers to the question.

- If possible, work the question before looking at the answer choices. Then look for your answer among the given choices. If your answer is not one of the choices, read the question again. Be sure that you understand the problem. Remember, common errors are often used to generate incorrect answer choices. Be sure you work carefully.

- Make sure you answer the question being asked. A partial answer to the question may be used as an incorrect answer choice.

- Always read **aii** of the possible answer choices—even if the first one seems like the correct answer. There may be a better choice farther down in the list.

- Think of what you already know about the math topic involved and use that information to help eliminate answer choices. You can also use estimation to eliminate answer choices.

- If you cannot work the question, you may be able to substitute the answer choices back into the question to find the correct choice. Start with the middle value. If the result is too large, then substitute a smaller value. If the result is too small, then substitute a larger value.

- Never leave a question blank. There is no penalty for guessing, so always choose an answer.

- When you are finished, reread the question and the selected answer to be sure that you made the best choice and that you marked it correctly on the answer sheet.

Tips for Answering Gridded-Response Questions

- Work the problem and find an answer. Then write your answer in the grid provided. There is often more than one correct way to write your answer in the response grid. Write out your answer in the top boxes first, then fill in the grid.

- When filling in your grid, make your marks heavy and dark. Fill in the circles completely, but do not shade outside the circles. Do not make any stray marks on or outside of your grid.

- If your answer does not fit in the grid, you may need to write your answer in another form. If your answer still does not fit, read the question again. Be sure that you understand the problem. Check your work for possible errors.

- It is not important where you place your answer in the answer boxes, as long as your entire answer fits.

- You may include a zero before the decimal point for decimals less than one, but it is not necessary.

- DO NOT:
  - Place spaces between the digits or symbols in the answer boxes.
  - Enter commas in numbers that have four or more digits.
  - Fill in a circle below an empty answer box.
  - Fill in more than one circle below each answer box in which you have written a number or symbol.

- Practice filling in sample answer grids so that you are used to the format.

- Check that your answer is reasonable by estimation, or try substituting the answer back in to the question or solving by another method.

- If you have time at the end of the test, go back and check again that your grids are filled properly.

Tips for Answering Extended-Response Questions

- Read the question first for its general intent and then reread it carefully. Make sure you understand exactly what is being asked. There is often more than one answer required, especially for extended-response questions.

- Use correct mathematical vocabulary and your best handwriting when answering the problem. Circle your answer.

- Show all work to get full credit. If you do a step in your head, write in words what you did and why.

- If you are unable to finish the problem, you may be able to get partial credit by writing down any information that you would use in solving the problem.

- If there is a figure accompanying the question, review the figure carefully. Read the labels and make sure you understand what the figure represents. Remember, a figure may not be drawn to scale.

- If a figure or graph is required in the answer, be sure that you draw the figure as accurately as possible and label all required parts.

- Never leave a question blank. There is no penalty for guessing, so always write an answer.

- When you are finished, reread the question. Check to make sure you answered all parts of the question.

Strategies for Success

There are various strategies you can employ ahead of time to help you feel more confident about answering questions on math standardized tests. Here are a few suggestions:

1. VISUALS

Note the labels on the charts and graphs. For example, a scale on one axis may provide a valuable clue. Read all graphs twice.

When reading diagrams, read all labels and tick marks carefully, and read diagrams twice, also.

Label the figure with any information stated in the problem that is not in the diagram. Use the properties of the figure, for example, if it is stated that a figure is a square, you can label all the sides with the same length.

If a figure is not provided, it may be helpful to draw one. Be sure that you do not assume any information that is not included in the problem. Remember, the figure does not have to look perfect. It is only to help you understand the relationships in the problem.

2. CONCEPTS

When answering questions about math concepts, don't let a hard question stump you. You can always work with what you do know. It's possible to answer a question when you know only a part of the concept being tested.

Another strategy to help you on difficult questions is to draw or sketch out the question's concept. Often you can understand how to answer a question by listing what you know, sketching the process, and then identifying what you are supposed to solve.

If you do not understand a problem on the test, try to relate it to a problem you can solve. For example, you can substitute simpler numbers into a problem and figure out how to solve it. Then try again with the original values in the problem.

3. MATH SKILLS

To help you on the math sections of the tests, practice the skills as you are reading and discussing your textbook. For example, you could put the steps to a process in order in your mind. Also, sequencing a process can become a game you play with a friend who also has to take the test. Always ask yourself what the most important points are when studying sections. Some of the more common skills for studying math are

- **Analyzing Information**—the process of breaking something down into its parts and examining the relationships between them. Analyzing enables you to better understand the whole.

- **Sequencing**—the process of placing the steps in a process in order to better understand the steps and the process as a whole. When you analyze the sequence, you are determining what happens first, second, and so on.

- **Categorizing**—the process by which you group things together by the characteristics they have in common. Categorizing helps you to make comparisons and see differences among things.

- **Identifying Cause and Effect**—interpreting the relationships between events. A *cause* makes something happen. An *effect* is what happens as a result of the cause.

- **Comparing and Contrasting**—the process of examining situations or ideas, etc., for their similarities and differences.

- **Summarizing**—the process of taking a large amount of information and boiling it down into a short clear statement. To *summarize* a problem, you must analyze the problem to find the most important points and the supporting information.

- **Paraphrasing**—a paraphrase is a restatement of someone's ideas or words. A paraphrase is usually about as long as the original; the ideas are just expressed in simpler terms. A paraphrase question might be stated like this, "According to the passage, which of these statements is accurate?"

- **Visualizing**—visualizing helps you see processes and procedures in your mind's eye. Visualizing will help you be successful on a variety of math questions you could encounter on tests.

4. READING MATH

First, remember that what you have learned about math can help you in answering comprehension questions on tests. Also, though, remember the following points:

- Read the problem as if you were not taking a test.

- Look at the big picture. Ask yourself questions like, *What is the question being asked? What do the diagrams or graphs tell me?*

- Read the problem quickly first. This technique will help you know what information to look for as you read.

- Reread the problem and underline information related to the questions.

- Go back to the question and try to answer it in your mind before looking at the answers.

- Read all the answer choices and eliminate the ones that are obviously incorrect.

- If you can eliminate certain answers, getting the choice down to two, go ahead and pick one of the two responses. That's an educated guess, and you are most likely better off making the choice.

Analyzing Word Problems

Many students who are comfortable with basic skill problems are still stumped by word problems. These steps will help you work through word problems on standardized tests.

Step 1 Understand the problem

Read the problem carefully and make sure you understand what is being asked. You may wish to rewrite the question in your own words.

List the given information or circle it in your test booklet, if you are allowed to write in it. Cross out any unnecessary information.

Step 2 Make a plan

Think about similar problems you have seen in the past, and how you solved them.

Determine a strategy or strategies that you will use to solve the problem, such as drawing a diagram, working backward, finding a pattern, or other problem-solving strategies.

Step 3 Solve the problem

Solve the problem according to your plan. If the strategy you chose is not working, go back and revise. Write out all the steps on your scratch paper to avoid making careless mistakes.

Step 4 Look Back

Make sure you answered the question that was asked.

Check your answer in the words of the problem to make sure your answer is reasonable.

Make sure your answer is in the correct place on the answer document.

Learning Math Vocabulary

Learning vocabulary is important in order to be successful on standardized tests. During the test, you will not be able to ask the meaning of a word, and you may not be able to answer a question that contains a word you do not know.

Spend time learning vocabulary throughout the year so that you are prepared for your test when the time comes.

Identify important terms:

As you learn new concepts, keep a list of unfamiliar terms. Also, review the standards for your grade and write down any words you do not know.

Learn the meaning of each term:

Look up the meaning of each new word in your glossary. It may help to use the Vocabulary Questioning Strategies shown on the next page. Another way to learn vocabulary is by using graphic organizers like the ones shown below.

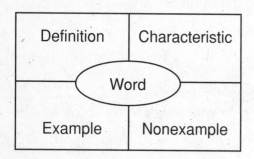

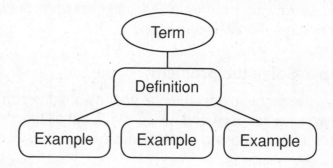

Memory aids:

Your lists of words may be used as memory aids, or it may be helpful to create flashcards with the term on the front and the definition and/or examples on the back. Review the flashcards frequently. As you learn the words, you may remove the flashcards from your stack, but keep them for occasional review before your exam.

Use context clues:

If you do encounter an unfamiliar word on your test, don't panic. Try to relate it to a familiar word or use context clues to determine the meaning of the word in the problem.

Vocabulary Questioning Strategies

Vocabulary term _____

Before you look up the word, predict its meaning. Some clues you can use are as follows:

- the way you have seen or heard the word used
- the everyday meaning of the word
- the meaning of the root word, prefix, or suffix

I think this word means _____

Look up the word in your glossary, and write its meaning here.

Write a question in your own words that contains the vocabulary term, and write the answer.

Question: _____

Answer: _____

Think of a strategy to remember the meaning of the word. Some possible strategies are as follows: draw a picture that represents the word, write a poem or song about the word, or relate the math meaning to the everyday meaning of the word. Write your strategy here.

Troubleshooting

Taking practice tests can be helpful, but you will get more out of them if you analyze the tests after they have been scored to see where you made mistakes. Look at the table below to see some common types of mistakes. Use the blank rows to add in your own types with how you can avoid them in the future.

Type of mistake	Ways to avoid it in the future
I was unfamiliar with the concept involved in the question.	Review the standards to make sure I know what will be covered on the test.
I knew how to do the problem, but I couldn't remember.	Maintain skills throughout the year. Review old tests and homework to keep old topics fresh.
I misread the problem.	Read the problem carefully, and check my answer against the words of the problem to make sure the answer makes sense.
I did not know the meaning of a word in the problem.	Make lists of vocabulary terms and use vocabulary strategies to learn their meanings.
I did not transfer the answer to the answer sheet correctly.	Check frequently that the answers are in the right place. Circle the answer in the answer booklet or on scratch paper so I can go back and check it.

xviii

NUMBER SENSE

Exponents and Roots

6.11.07 Determine the effects of operations on the magnitude of quantities (e.g., multiplication, division, powers, roots). III.B.6

Select the best answer for each question.

1. Which of the following is equal to 4^{-3}?

   A. $\dfrac{1}{4^3}$

   B. $\dfrac{1}{16}$

   C. 16

   D. 64

2. The volume of a particular cube is 1,728 cubic inches. What is the length of an edge of the cube, in inches?

   A. 10

   B. 11

   C. 12

   D. 13

3. A number to the 17th power divided by the same number to the 14th power equals 343. What is the number?

   A. 3

   B. 5

   C. 7

   D. 8

4. Simplify.

   $$4^2 + 9 \cdot \left(3^{-2}\right)$$

   A. 12

   B. 17

   C. 18

   D. 32

5. Which of the following is equal to 7^4?

   A. $7^3 \times 7^1$

   B. 49^2

   C. 2,401

   D. All of the above

6. In 2006, the population of Jacksonville, FL, was 773,781. If the population doubles every 10 years, what will the population be in 2046?

   A. 3,210,553

   B. 6,190,248

   C. 15,475,620

   D. 12,380,496

7. $\sqrt{47}$ lies between which two consecutive integers?

   A. 5 and 6

   B. 6 and 7

   C. 7 and 8

   D. 8 and 9

8. Angie's math teacher asked her to name an irrational number close to 8. Which of these numbers would be best for her to name?

A. $\sqrt[3]{514}$

B. $\sqrt[3]{498}$

C. $\sqrt[3]{450}$

D. $\sqrt[3]{64}$

9. Order, from least to greatest.

A. $6^2, \sqrt{10}, \sqrt[3]{343}, 35.2, \sqrt{37}$

B. $\sqrt{37}, \sqrt[3]{343}, \sqrt{10}, 35.2, 6^2$

C. $\sqrt{37}, 6^2, \sqrt{10}, 3R343, 35.2$

D. $\sqrt{10}, \sqrt{37}, \sqrt[3]{343}, 35.2, 6^2$

10. The cube root of a number is $\frac{1}{2}$ of 8×6. What is the number?

A. 12,368

B. 18,324

C. 13,824

D. 13,838

11. The distance from Earth to the moon is 22^4 mi. The distance from Earth to Neptune is about 22^7 mi. How many one-way trips from Earth to the moon are equal to 1 trip from Earth to Neptune?

A. 10

B. 3^{22}

C. 22^3

D. 50

Gridded-Response: Fill in the grid with your answer to each question.

12. Find the cube root of 17.

13. The formula $D = 3.56 \cdot \sqrt{A}$ gives the distance D in kilometers to the horizon from an airplane flying at an altitude A in meters. If a pilot is flying at an altitude of 2,000 m, about how far away is the horizon in kilometers?

Extended-Response: Show your work.

14. A carpenter wants to use as many of her 224 small wood squares as possible to make a large square box lid. How many squares will she have left over after making the lid?

MN Test Prep Grade 9

NUMBER SENSE

Order of Operations

6.11.04 Apply the rules of order of operations to real-number expressions. II.B.1

Select the best answer for each question.

1. Use the order of operations to simplify.

$$95 \div (8 - 3) - (3 \times 0.6)^2$$

A. 2.635
B. 7.84
C. 15.76
D. 22.8

2. Which operation should be performed first to simplify the following expression?

$$9(8 - 6)^2 \div 4$$

A. Subtraction
B. Multiplication
C. Division
D. Squaring

3. Which operation symbol would make this expression correct?

$$10 \times 5 \; \square \; 8 \times 4 = 82$$

A. –
B. +
C. ×
D. ÷

4. Use the order of operations to simplify.

$$96 \div 2(12 + 4) - 33$$

A. −30
B. 36
C. 741
D. 768

5. Rick spent \$20/ft^2 for carpet and \$30 for carpet padding. Simplify $30 + 20(12^2 \div 9)$ to find out how much Rick spent in all to carpet a 12 ft^2 room.

A. \$212
B. \$350
C. \$562
D. \$791

6. Which operation should be performed second to simplify the following expression?

$$92 \div (3 \times 8)^2 - 18$$

A. Subtraction
B. Multiplication
C. Squaring
D. Division

7. The math club is selling t-shirts. They have sold 8 medium and 16 large t-shirts. Which expression shows how much the math club has earned so far?

Price of T-Shirts	
Medium	\$8.75
Large	\$9.25
Extra Large	\$10.25

A. $(8 + 16)(8.75 + 9.25)$
B. $8 \times 8.75 + 16 \times 9.25$
C. $(8 \times 16) + (8.75 \times 9.25)$
D. $(8 \times 8.75)(16 \times 9.25)$

MN Test Prep Grade 9

8. Which placement of the parentheses makes the statement true?

A. $51 + \left(3 \times 8^2\right) - 191 = 52$

B. $(51 + 3) \times 8^2 - 191 = 52$

C. $51 + 3 \times \left(8^2 - 191\right) = 52$

D. $51 + (3 \times 8)^2 - 191 = 52$

9. Use the order of operations to simplify.

$$4(8) \div 2\left(15 - 3^2\right)$$

A. $1\dfrac{1}{3}$

B. $2\dfrac{2}{3}$

C. 48

D. $\dfrac{1}{9}$

Gridded-Response: Fill in the grid with your answer to each question.

10. Use the order of operations to simplify.

$$38 \div 2 + \sqrt{81} \times 4 - 31$$

11. Use the order of operations to simplify.

$$27 \div (3 + 6) + 62$$

Extended-Response: Show your work.

12. Antwaan simplified this expression:

$$(12 - 4 + 6 \times 2 - 8)^2 = 121$$

Is his math correct?

13. Sadowski Produce has 9 employees. Each employee works 28 hours per week and earns $9.25 per hour. The company has to send 11% of its payroll to the government for taxes.

A. Write an expression that shows how much money the company should send to the government each week.

B. Calculate the amount.

NUMBER SENSE

Absolute Value

6.11.16 Simplify numerical problems involving absolute value. II.A.1

Select the best answer for each question.

1. The number line shows the absolute values of which numbers?

- **A.** 4 and −4
- **B.** −2 and 2
- **C.** 0 and 2
- **D.** −2 and −4

2. What integer is described below?

The absolute value of this number is 5, and the number lies to the left of 0 on the number line.

- **A.** −5
- **B.** $\sqrt{-5}$
- **C.** |−5|
- **D.** 5

3. Ships that travel from Lake Erie to Lake Ontario pass through the Welland Canal. At Lock 2, the ship was at −81.2 feet compared to the level of Lake Erie. At Lock 6, the ship was at −244.875 feet compared to the level of Lake Erie. What is the change in altitude between Lock 2 and Lock 6?

- **A.** 163.675 feet
- **B.** |326.075| feet
- **C.** −326.075 feet
- **D.** −163.675 feet

4. The chart shows the change in the value of some stocks. Which stock showed the greatest change?

Stock	Value	Change
ABC Corporation	$52.93	+$3.42
BiggieMart	$74.16	−$1.98
GoCar Company	$61.98	−$8.13
FlyRight Airline	$12.55	+$0.45

- **A.** ABC Corporation
- **B.** BiggieMart
- **C.** GoCar Company
- **D.** FlyRight Airline

5. The Cougars football team started on the 30-yard line and fell back to the 19-yard line. Which represents the change in their position?

- **A.** |−11| yards
- **B.** |11| yards
- **C.** 11 yards
- **D.** −|30 − 19| yards

6. What number is the opposite of |−8|?

- **A.** −|8|
- **B.** |8|
- **C.** 8
- **D.** All of the above

7. What is the value of the expression $52 - |{-15}|$?

  A. 15
  B. 37
  C. 47
  D. 69

8. Simplify the expression $|16| - 2|{-3}|$.

  A. 10
  B. 16
  C. 19
  D. 22

9. The chart shows the submarine's depth for four hours. Which expression can be used to find the amount of the greatest change after the first hour?

Time	1 A.M.	2 A.M.	3 A.M.	4 A.M.
Depth (m)	−80	−204	−137	−171

  A. $-80 - (-204)$ meters
  B. $-80 + (-204)$ meters
  C. $-80 + |{-204}|$ meters
  D. $-204 - |{-80}|$ meters

10. The summit of Mount Everest is 29,035 feet above sea level. The Mariana Trench is below sea level, at −36,201 feet. Which expression could be used to find the change in elevation between these two locations?

  A. $-|36{,}201| - 29{,}035$
  B. $|{-36{,}201}| + |29{,}035|$
  C. $|{-36{,}201 + 29{,}035}|$
  D. $-36{,}201 + |29{,}035|$

Gridded-Response: Fill in the grid with your answer to each question.

11. The chart shows the temperature at noon in Portland, Maine, and the change from the previous day. Which is the greatest amount of change?

Day	1	2	3	4	5
Temp.	2°	6°	−3°	0	−8°
Degrees Change	0°	+4°	−9°	+3°	−8°

Extended-Response: Show your work.

12. A skydiver jumped out of an airplane at 7000 feet above ground level. He landed on a hill 84 feet above ground level. Write an expression that shows the distance between the skydiver's jumping point and the landing.

MN Test Prep Grade 9

ALGEBRA

Algebraic Expressions

8.11.01 Simplify or identify equivalent algebraic expressions (e.g., exponential, rational, logarithmic, factored, polynomial). Also 8.11.02, 8.11.06, III.B.1

Select the best answer for each question.

1. Which of the following is the correct translation of 9 less than p?

   A. $p + 9$

   B. $9 + p$

   C. $p - 9$

   D. $9 - p$

2. Which expression represents the verbal phrase "the sum of three times a number and five"?

   A. $3(n + 5)$

   B. $3 + n \times 5$

   C. $3 + (n + 5)$

   D. $3n + 5$

3. Which of the following is equivalent to this expression?

$$-35x - 5$$

   A. $-7x + 1$

   B. $-5(7x + 1)$

   C. $5(8x + 1)$

   D. $x(-35 - 5)$

4. Simplify $\dfrac{3\sqrt{6^2 + 8^2}}{5}$.

   A. 6

   B. 10

   C. 14

   D. 30

5. Evaluate $x^3 - 2x^2 + 5x - 10$ when x equals 3.

   A. 14

   B. 15

   C. -10

   D. -14

6. What is the equivalent form for this expression? $(x + 5)(x + 2)$

   A. $x^2 + 2x + 5$

   B. $7x^2 + 2x + 5$

   C. $2x^2 + 7x + 5$

   D. $x^2 + 7x + 10$

7. Hector has 6 times as many coins as Joan. If Hector has 126 coins, which expression would you use to find out how many coins Joan has?

   A. $\dfrac{6}{126}$

   B. $\dfrac{126}{6}$

   C. $6(126)$

   D. $\dfrac{126 + 6}{6}$

8. Which value of h makes the statement true?

$\frac{3}{4}(24 + 8h)$ is equivalent to $2(5h + 1)$.

A. 2

B. $2\frac{3}{4}$

C. 1

D. $\frac{17}{4}$

9. Amber is asked to simplify the following expression.

$4\,t^3 - 5t + 12\,t^2 - 12 + (3\,t^4 + t^2 - 12t + 15)$

After she finishes simplifying, what should the coefficient of the t term be?

A. 17

B. −7

C. −5

D. 7

10. Patsy writes an expression that will always represent an odd number. Which expression did she write?

A. $m + 1$

B. $2m + 1$

C. m^2

D. $m^2 + 1$

11. The cost of a long distance call is $2.50 for the first three minutes and $0.10 for each additional minute. Theo called home and talked for 8 minutes. How much is he going to be charged?

A. $2.50

B. $2.90

C. $3.00

D. $3.50

Use the information to answer questions 12 and 13.

A Great Copy Center sent Chelie the following invoice for her latest order.

No. of Copies	Price per Copy	Subtotal
c	$0.05	x
	Processing Fee	$3.00
	Total	$15.80

12. Which expression is equal to x?

A. $15.80 ÷ $3.00

B. $15.80 − $3.00

C. $15.80 + $3.00

D. $15.80 × $3.00

13. Find the value of c.

A. 132

B. 157

C. 232

D. 256

14. Use the formula for compound interest, $A = C(1 + r)^t$, where A is the account balance, r is the rate and C is the initial amount. Approximate the balance when the initial value is $500, the time is 6 years and the rate is 0.08. Round to the nearest whole number.

   A. $280

   B. $623

   C. $793

   D. $3240

Gridded-Response: Fill in the grid with your answer to each question.

15. The formula for the area of a trapezoid is $A = \frac{1}{2}(B + b)h$, where B is the larger base, b is the smaller base and h is the height. Find the area of a trapezoid that has one base of 18.2 inches, the other base of 14 inches and a height of 8 inches.

16. A formula for a child's dosage C of medication is given by $C = \left(\frac{A}{A + 12}\right)D$ where A is the child's age and D is the adult dosage. Find D if $C = 60$ and $A = 6$ years?

Evaluate the expressions in questions 15 and 16 when $y = 3$.

17. $50 - y^3 \times 5$

18. $3 + [(13 - y) \times 21]$

Extended-Response: Show your work.

19. Sarah's hourly charge for babysitting is $5.50, plus $0.25 for each child she supervises.

   A. Write an expression for determining the hourly charge if Sarah supervises c children.

   B. Write an expression for determining the total amount she would earn if she supervises c children for h hours and receives a $5 tip at the end of the evening.

   C. For which job will Sarah earn more money: supervising 3 children for 4 hours in one evening, or supervising 1 child for 2 hours each evening for 2 evenings? Assume she receives a $5 tip at the end of each evening. Explain your answer.

MN Test Prep Grade 9

ALGEBRA

Patterns, Sequences, and Functions

> 8.11.04 Determine aspecific term, a finite sum, or a rule that generates terms of a pattern. III.B.5

Select the best answer for each question.

1. Study the pattern below. Which choice gives the next five terms of this pattern?

   $ $ W $ $ W W $ $ W W W ...

   A. W W W W $
   B. $ W W W W
   C. W W $ $ W
   D. $ $ W W W

2. What number appears in the 4th position of the given pattern?

   2 4 6 8 9 2 4 6 8 9 2 4 6 8 9 2 4 6 8 9

   A. 4
   B. 2
   C. 6
   D. 8

3. A number that repeats after the decimal point is a rational number. A number that has a pattern but does not repeat after the decimal point is an irrational number. Which of the following is an irrational number?

   A. 3.33333...
   B. 3.03030303...
   C. 3.13113111311113
   D. 3.$\overline{027}$

4. Which of the following sequences has a pattern?

   A. 35, 41, 47, 53, 59
   B. 24, 26, 28, 25, 24
   C. 20, 19, 22, 25, 28
   D. 15, 19, 23, 27, 30

5. Describe how the terms change in the following sequence.

   5, 7, 11, 17, 25, ...

   A. The terms increase by a power of 2.
   B. The terms increase by an odd number.
   C. The terms increase by 2, then increase by 4, increase by 2, then 4.
   D. The terms increase by consecutive even numbers.

6. What would you do to go from one term to the next term?

   300, 60, 12, ...

   A. Divide by 300
   B. Divide by 5
   C. Divided by 2
   D. Subtract a power of 3

10

7. Complete the table for the missing value.

x	1	2	3	4	5
y	1	8	27	64	??

A. 25

B. 50

C. 125

D. 250

8. Which of the following is considered a pattern?

A.

B.

C.

D. □○●▽▼□○●△▲
   □●▽□○●▽▼

9. The first few values of a function are shown in the table below.

n	1	2	3	4	5
f(n)	4	7	10	13	16

Which expression gives an expression for $f(n)$ that is consistent with the information in the table?

A. $n + 3$

B. $3n$

C. $3n + 1$

D. $4n$

10. If Tom gets $2 from his father daily, how much will he have on the 10th day?

A. $20   C. $30

B. $22   D. $18

11. If this pattern is continued, how many shaded triangles will be in Level 4?

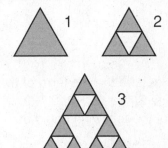

A. 20   C. 23

B. 22   D. 27

12. What is the pattern for the given sequence?

6.5, 42.25, 274.625, 1785.0625, …

A. Multiply by 6.5

B. Multiply by 6.2

C. Add 37.75

D. Multiply by 3.375

MN Test Prep Grade 9

Name_____ Date_____ Class_____

13. The first few values of a function are shown in the table below.

n	1	2	3	4	5
$f(n)$	−2	−3	−4	−5	−6

Which expression gives an expression for $f(n)$ that is consistent with the information in the table?

A. $−n − 1$

B. $−2n$

C. $−n + 1$

D. $n − 3$

14. Let $f(n)$ denote the nth term of the sequence 2, −2, 2, −2, 2, −2, ... Which of the following could be true?

A. $f(n) = −2(−1)^n$

B. $f(n) = 2(−1)^n$

C. $f(n) = (−2)^n$

D. $f(n) = −(−2)^n$

15. The first day Corey opened a savings account with $100. Each day, Corey would deposit or withdraw money from the account according to a special rule. If the number of dollars in the account was even, then Corey would add $11. If the number of dollars in the account was odd, then Corey would subtract $5. Let $a(d)$ denote the amount of money in the account after d days. Which of the following statements is true?

A. $a(d)$ is not a function of d.

B. $a(d)$ is a function of d.

C. $a(d)$ is not well-defined.

D. $a(1) = 200$

Gridded-Response: Fill in the grid with your answer to each question.

16. A sequence is given by the function $f(n) = n + 6$. What is $f(15)$?

Extended-Response: Show your work.

17. Look at the pattern of diagonals. How many diagonals does an octagon have?

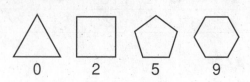

0   2   5   9

18. The function $y = 31,000(0.98^x)$ models the population of Purpleton x years from now.

A. Explain the meaning of the function in terms of the current population and the growth rate.

B. The population of Verdon is currently equal to the population of Purpleton. The population of Verdon is increasing by 3% each year. Write a function that models the population of Verdon x years from now, and compare it to the function that models the population of Purpleton.

MN Test Prep Grade 9

ALGEBRA

Relations and Functions

8.11.14 Model problems using mathematical functions and relations (e.g., linear, non-linear). Also, 8.11.21, III.A.5

Select the best answer for each question.

1. Which of the following is a linear function?

   A. $y = x^2$

   B. $y = 2^x$

   C. $y = 2x$

   D. None of the above

2. Which of the following is a function?

   A. $y = x^2$

   B. $y = 2^x$

   C. $y = 2x$

   D. All of the above

3. Can you tell if a relation is also a function by just looking at the graph of the equation?

   A. Yes

   B. No

   C. Only when it is a function

   D. Only when it is not a function

4. Name the model that the graph of $y = \frac{1}{2}x^2 + 5$ represents.

   A. Quadratic

   B. Exponential

   C. Linear

   D. A and B are correct

5. What is the range of the following function?

   $$y = x^2$$

   A. All real numbers

   B. All integers

   C. All positive real numbers and 0

   D. All negative real numbers and 0

6. What is the domain of the following function?

   $$y = x$$

   A. All real numbers

   B. All integers

   C. All positive real numbers and 0

   D. All negative real numbers and 0

7. Which of the following statements is correct?

   A. The independent variable is on the y-axis.

   B. The independent variable is on the x-axis.

   C. The dependent variable is on the x-axis.

   D. The dependent variable is on the y-axis or x-axis.

8. Which of the following is a linear function?

   A. $y = 3x^2 + 2$

   B. $4y = 2^x - 2$

   C. $5y = 3x + 5$

   D. All of the above

9. Which of the following is a function?

   A. $y = 3x^2 + 2$

   B. $4y = 2^x - 2$

   C. $5y = 3x + 5$

   D. All of the above

10. Which of the following statements is correct?

   A. If y is a function then it is a relation.

   B. If y is a function, then y might be a relation.

   C. If y is a relation, then it is a function.

   D. y can be either a function or a relation.

11. Which of the following functions matches the data in the table?

x	y
2	3
3	8
4	15
5	24

   A. $y = x^2$

   B. $y = 3x$

   C. $y = x^2 - 1$

   D. $y = 3x - 1$

Gridded-Response: Fill in the grid with your answer to each question.

12. If $y = 2x + 7$, what is the value of y when $x = -3$?

Extended-Response: Show your work.

13. Consider the relation defined by the set of ordered pairs $\{(-2, 3), (-1, 4), (0, 1), (1, -4), (2, -4), (3, -2), (4,0)\}$

   A. Is this relation a function? Explain.

   B. You can find the inverse of this relation by switching the x- and y-coordinate in each ordered pair (e.g., $(-2, 3)$ becomes $(3, -2)$). Is the inverse of this relation a function? Explain your answer.

Name_____ Date _____ Class_____

ALGEBRA

Inequalities

9.A3.1 Model real-world phenomena using linear and quadratic equations and linear inequalities (e.g., apply algebraic techniques to solve rate problems, work problems, and percent mixture problems; solve problems that involve discounts, markups, commissions, and profit and compute simple and compound interest; apply quadratic equations to model throwing a baseball in the air). III.B.4

Select the best answer for each question.

1. Describe the solution of $3x \leq 21$.

  A. All real numbers less than 7

  B. All real numbers less than or equal to 7

  C. All real numbers greater than or equal to 7

  D. All real numbers greater than 7

2. Which graph represents the solution of $x + 6 > 8$?

  A.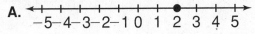

  B.

  C.

  D.

3. Which graph represents the solution of $-6 < x - 3 \leq -1$?

  A.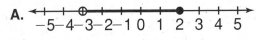

  B.

  C.

  D.

4. The graph on the number line below represents the solution to which inequality?

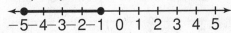

  A. $|w| \leq -1$

  B. $|w + 3| \leq 2$

  C. $|w| \geq 5$

  D. $|w + 3| \geq 2$

5. Which inequality describes the possible values of x?

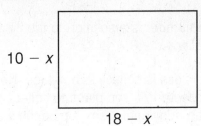

  A. $x > 10$

  B. $x < 10$

  C. $x > 18$

  D. $x < 18$

6. Describe the graph of the solution of $6x \geq 42$.

  A. Open dot on 7 and arrow pointing to the right

  B. Closed dot on 7 and arrow pointing to the left

  C. Closed dot on 7 and arrow pointing to the right

  D. Closed dot on 7

7. Which inequality represents all real numbers greater than 5 and less than or equal to 12?

A. $5 < x \le 12$

B. $5 \le x \le 12$

C. $5 < x < 12$

D. $5 < x$ or $x \ge 12$

8. Which graph represents the solution of the inequality $4x + 1 < 17$ or $3x - 11 \ge 10$?

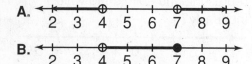

A.

B.

C.

D.

Gridded-Response: Fill in the grid with your answer to each question.

9. Which number is a solution to the inequality $4x + 8 < 24$?

10. Kelly's class is collecting box tops. Kelly has collected 75 and plans to collect at least an additional 4 box tops each week. The inequality $y \ge 75 + 4x$ can be used to represent this situation. At most, how many weeks will it take her to collect 119 box tops?

Extended-Response: Show your work.

11. There are 3 children in the Smith Family—Walter, Joanie, and Cole. Cole, the youngest child, is at least 5 years old. Walter, the oldest child, is less than 23 years old and older than twice Cole's age. Joanie is 3 years older than Cole.

A. Write an inequality to show Joanie's age. Explain your answer.

B. Write an inequality to show Walter's age. Explain your answer.

MN Test Prep Grade 9

ALGEBRA

Quadratic Equations

8.11.18 Solve quadratic equations over the complex number system, including selecting and evaluating formulas. Also 8.11.12, III.B.8

Select the best answer for each question.

1. Which of the following is the quadratic formula?

   A. $\dfrac{-b \pm \sqrt{b - 4ac}}{2a}$

   B. $\dfrac{-b \pm \sqrt{b^2 + 4ac}}{2a}$

   C. $\dfrac{-b \pm \sqrt{b^2 - 4ac}}{2a}$

   D. $-b \pm \dfrac{\sqrt{b^2 + 4ac}}{2a^2}$

2. Factoring $x^2 + 2x + 1$ will result in
   _____.

   A. $(x + 1)(x + 2)$
   B. $(x + 1)(x + 1)$
   C. $(x + 2)(x + 2)$
   D. $(x + 3)(x - 2)$

3. Expanding $(x + 2)(x + 3)$ will result in
   _____.

   A. $x^2 + 3x + 2$
   B. $x^2 + 2x + 1$
   C. $x^2 + 5x + 6$
   D. $x^2 - 5x + 6$

4. What are the roots in $x^2 + 6x + 9$?

   A. 3
   B. −3
   C. −2 and −14
   D. −0.205 and −14.795

5. What are the roots of the quadratic equation $y = x^2 + 10x + 21$?

   A. 5 and 6
   B. 3 and 7
   C. 3 and 9
   D. None of the above

6. Which of the following statements is FALSE?

   A. A root is when the dependent variable equals to 0.
   B. A quadratic equation always has 2 roots.
   C. Parabolas can be made only by quadratic equations.
   D. Quadratic equations have a degree of 3.

7. Which of the following is NOT a solution to the equation $y = x^2 + 2x + 4$?

   A. $(-1, 3)$

   B. $(1, 7)$

   C. $(2, 12)$

   D. $(3, 7)$

8. A certain type of bacteria has the following model to represent its population during an experiment: $p = t^2 + 14t + 5$, where p is the population in thousands and t is the time in hours. How many bacteria will be in the experiment 5 hours after it started?

   A. 100 thousand

   B. 200 thousand

   C. 150 thousand

   D. 40 thousand

9. The equation $h = -t^2 + 6t + 7$ gives the height h of the ball from the ground t seconds after the ball has been thrown. When will the ball hit the ground?

   A. After 3 seconds

   B. After 5 seconds

   C. After 7 seconds

   D. After 2 and after 4 seconds

10. If the equation $w = -x^2 + 6x$ models an animal's weight in x days after it is born, is it physically reasonable to discuss $w(8)$?

   A. Yes

   B. No

   C. Sometimes

   D. It cannot be determined.

11. The height in feet of a projectile is given by $-16t^2 + 100t + 8$, where t is time measured in seconds. Which equation can be used to determine at what time the projectile is 150 feet above the ground?

   A. $-16t^2 + 100t = 150$

   B. $-16t^2 + 100t + 8 = 150$

   C. $-16t^2 + 100t = 158$

   D. $-16t^2 + 100t + 158 = 0$

12. Travis is working on top of a roof. He asks his friend Carl to toss him a tool. The height of the tool above the ground is given by $-16t^2 + 32t + 4$, where t is time in seconds. Travis can catch the tool at any moment that it is at least 15 feet off the ground. Which equation can be used to determine the first and last times that Travis can catch the tool?

   A. $16t^2 - 32t + 11 = 0$

   B. $16t^2 + 32t + 11 = 0$

   C. $16t^2 - 32t + 15 = 0$

   D. To solve this problem, two different equations are required.

13. Which quadratic equation has exactly one solution?

   A. $x^2 - 2x = 0$

   B. $x^2 - 2x + 1 = 0$

   C. $x^2 + 1 = 0$

   D. $x^2 - 4x + 2 = 0$

14. Which quadratic equation has no real solution?

- **A.** $-x^2 - 4x + 20$
- **B.** $x^2 - 3x + 2 = 0$
- **C.** $3x^2 + 2x - 1 = 0$
- **D.** $2x^2 + 2x + 1 = 0$

Gridded-Response: Fill in the grid with your answer to each question.

15. Jones likes to collect stamps. The equation $b = 2(x - 3)^2 + 10$ models this habit, where b is the number of stamps collected for the day and x is the number of days after she started collecting. Which of the following value for x will result in the minimum value for b?

16. A rock is falling from the top of a building. Its velocity is modeled by the equation $v = -4.9\,t^2$, where v is the velocity in meters per second and t is the time in seconds. What will be the rock's velocity 10 seconds after it is dropped?

Extended-Response: Show your work.

17. The width of a rectangle is 3 more than 2 times the length.

- **A.** Let x be the length of the rectangle. Write a quadratic equation that represents the area A in terms of x. Explain your answer.

- **B.** Suppose the area of the rectangle is 20 cm^2. Explain the relationship of the solutions of the quadratic equation to the dimensions of the rectangle.

ALGEBRA

Systems of Equations

9.A3.4 Express the relationship between two variables using an equation and a graph: graph a linear equation and linear inequality in two variables; solve linear inequalities and equations in one variable; solve systems of linear equations in two variables and graph the solutions; use the graph of a system of equations in two variables to help determine the solution. Also 9.A3.8, III.B.II

Select the best answer for each question.

1. Let (a, b) be the solution to the system of linear equations $x + y = 10$ and $7x - y = -2$. What is b?

   A. 3
   B. 6
   C. 9
   D. 12

2. The graph of two linear equations is shown below.

   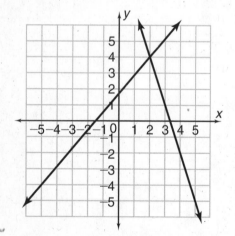

   Based on the graph, what is a solution to both linear equations?

   A. (2, 3)
   B. (3, 2)
   C. (1, 4)
   D. (2, 4)

3. The numbers x and y simultaneously satisfy $x - y = -4$ and $2x - y = 0$. What is $x + y$?

   A. 2
   B. 8
   C. 12
   D. 15

4. To solve the following system of equations by elimination, which operation would you perform first?

   $2.45x + 0.65y = 9.95$
   $6.25x + 0.65y = 21.35$

   A. Addition
   B. Subtraction
   C. Multiplication
   D. Division

5. At what point (x, y) do the two lines with equations $x - 2y = 5$ and $3x - 5y = 8$ intersect?

   A. $(-9, 7)$
   B. $\left(2, -\frac{3}{2}\right)$
   C. $\left(-2, -\frac{7}{2}\right)$
   D. $(-9, -7)$

6. Choose the statement that is true for a system of two linear equations.

   A. A system can only be solved by graphing the equations.

   B. There are infinitely many solutions when the graphs of the equations have the same slope and intercepts.

   C. There is exactly one solution when the graphs of the equations are one line.

   D. When solving a system by substitution the first step is to add the equations.

7. A farmer raises apples and peaches on 215 acres of land. If he wants to plant 31 more acres in apples than peaches, how many acres of each should he plant? Which system of equations will help determine how many acres of each he should plant?

   A. $a + p = 215$
      $a + p = 31$

   C. $a + p = 215$
      $a - p = 31$

   B. $a - p = 215$
      $a + p = 31$

   D. $a - p = 215$
      $a - p = 31$

8. Which ordered pair is a solution of the system $\begin{aligned}2x + y &= -5\\ 3x + 5y &= -4\end{aligned}$?

   A. $(-3, 1)$

   C. $(0, -5)$

   B. $(3, 1)$

   D. $(2, -1)$

9. To solve the following system of equations by elimination, which step would you perform first?

$$10a + 6b = 8$$
$$5a + 3b = 2$$

   A. Add the two equations.

   B. Subtract the two equations.

   C. Multiply both equations by -2.

   D. Multiply equation 2 by -2.

Gridded-Response: Fill in the grid with your answer to each question.

10. What is the value of x in the system of equations?

$$5x = 4y - 7$$
$$8y = 6x + 2$$

Extended-Response: Show your work.

11. The slope-intercept form of a line is $y = mx + b$.

   A. Explain how you could use the slope-intercept form to write a system of equations to find the equation of the line through $(1, 3)$ and $(5, 5)$.

   B. Explain how you could use the method from part A to write a formula for the equation of the line through the points (x_1, y_1) and (x_2, y_2).

ALGEBRA

Linear Functions

9.A3.7 Create a linear equation from a table of values containing co-linear data. III.A.1

Select the best answer for each question.

1. What is the slope of the linear function shown in the table?

x	1	3	6	8
y	5	1	−5	−9

   A. −2

   B. 2

   C. 4

   D. 7

2. Which graph does not represent a linear function?

   A.
   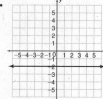

   C.
   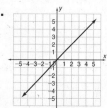

   B.
   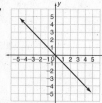

   D.
   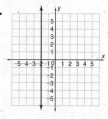

3. The graph of a linear function passes through the point (2, 4). For which value of the slope does the graph have a *y*-intercept of −6?

   A. −1

   B. 1

   C. 2

   D. 5

4. What is the *x*-intercept of the linear function $f(x) = -3x + 6$?

   A. −2

   B. 2

   C. 3

   D. 6

5. For what value of x does $f(x) = -\frac{2}{3}x + 5$ have a *y*-value of 7?

   A. −6

   B. −3

   C. 3

   D. 6

6. Complete the table for the missing value.

x	1	2	3	4	5
y	1	8	27	64	??

A. 25   **C.** 125

B. 50   **D.** 250

Gridded-Response: Fill in the grid with your answer to each question.

7. You are in charge of buying bags of pretzels and popcorn for the school picnic. A bag of pretzels costs $3.00 and a bag of popcorn costs $4. You have $48 to spend. What is the value of m in the table?

Popcorn	Pretzels
0	16
3	12
6	8
9	m
12	0

Use the table for question 8.

x	y
3	9
6	18
9	27
12	36

8. What *y*-value corresponds to an *x*-value of 7?

Extended-Response: Show your work.

9.

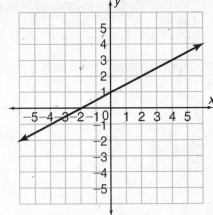

A. If the *x*-intercept in the graph were to stay the same and the slope of the line decreased, what impact would that have on the *y*-intercept? Explain your answer.

B. If the *y*-intercept in the graph were to stay the same and the *x*-intercept increased, what impact would that have on the slope of the line? Explain your answer.

ALGEBRA

Exponential Functions

> 8.11.19 Solve problems that include nonlinear functions, including selecting and evaluating formulas (i.e., absolute value, trigonometric, logarithmic, exponential). Also 8.11.03, III.B.6

Select the best answer for each question.

1. Simplify: $\dfrac{5\sqrt{\dfrac{7}{3} + \dfrac{2^2}{9}}}{-2}$

   A. $\dfrac{1}{6}$

   B. $-\dfrac{5}{6}$

   C. $-\dfrac{25}{6}$

   D. $\dfrac{40}{6}$

2. Which of the following is an exponential function?

   A. $y = x$

   B. $y = 4$

   C. $y = 3^x$

   D. $y = x^3$

3. Which of the following is NOT an example of an exponential function?

   A. $f(x) = \sqrt{x}$

   B. $f(x) = 3^x$

   C. $f(x) = -1^x$

   D. $f(x) = (-1)^x$

4. In the function $f(x) = 2^x$ if a positive value of x is increased by 1, what is the effect on the value of the function?

   A. It is $\dfrac{1}{2}$ the original amount.

   B. It is equal to the original amount.

   C. It is one more than the original amount.

   D. None of the above

5. According to the function,

$y = 3x\left(\dfrac{3}{5}x + 2^x\right)$, what is

the y value when $x = 7$:

   A. 2,789

   B. 2,776.2

   C. 555.3

   D. 6,268.1

6. $f(x) = 5^{x + 4 - 7x}$ is equivalent to

_____.

   A. $f(x) = 5^x + 5^4 - 5^{7x}$

   B. $f(x) = 5^x 5^4 - 5^{7x}$

   C. $f(x) = 5^x 5^4 5^{7x}$

   D. $f(x) = \dfrac{5^x 5^4}{5^{7x}}$

7. A certain chemical substance has a half-life of 2,000 years. A scientist currently has 100 g of that substance. After 6,000 years, how much of the substance will be left even if the scientist uses none of it?

   A. 12.5 g   **C.** 17 g

   B. 25 g   **D.** 28 g

8. Certain bacteria can double in number over 1 hour. Suppose the collection of 60 bacteria cells are placed in a Petri dish. What expression can be used to find how many cells, c, there would there be after x hours?

   A. $c = 60x * 2$

   B. $c = 60 * x^2$

   C. $c = 60 * 2^x$

   D. $c = 60x * 2$

9. What is the y-intercept for all of the exponential functions given that the base is positive and that the function takes the form of $y = a^{bx}$?

   A. 1

   B. 2

   C. 0

   D. The y-intercept is undefined.

10. Which function will increase faster for positive x values?

   One: $y = 3^x$

   Two: $y = 5^x$

   A. One

   B. Two

   C. The functions wil increase at the rate.

   D. Neither function is increasing.

Gridded-Response: Fill in the grid with your answer to each question.

11. Evaluate $y = 5^x + 3^x$ for $x = 3$.

12. A half life function would have _____ as it base.

Extended-Response: Show your work.

13. Can the equation $y = \dfrac{4^x + 3^x}{5^x}$ be simplified further? Explain your answer.

ALGEBRA

Linear and Nonlinear Functions

> 8.11.03 Identify essential quantitative relationships in a situation, and determine the class or classes of functions (e.g., linear, quadratic, exponential) that model the relationships. Also 8.11.05, 8.11.08, 8.11.09, 8.11.11, 8.11.12, 8.11.19, III.A.4

Select the best answer for each question.

1. A linear function has a degree of one. Is this statement correct?

   A. Yes

   B. No

   C. Sometimes

   D. It cannot be determined.

2. In the equation $m = -22b + 13$, which relationship between m and b is true?

   A. b is dependent on m.

   B. m and b are independent of each other.

   C. m is dependent on b.

   D. There is no relationship between m and b.

3. Solve the equation for n.

   $$\frac{1}{4}n - \frac{1}{8}n = 3 - \frac{1}{16}n$$

   A. $n = \frac{7}{3}$

   B. $n = 3$

   C. $n = 8$

   D. $n = 16$

4. For the equation $y = -4x + 7$, what is the slope and the y-intercept?

   A. $-4, 3$

   B. $-4, -7$

   C. $-4, 7$

   D. $4, 7$

5. $2y - 3x = 7$ is equivalent to

   A. $y = 3x + 7$

   B. $y = \frac{3}{2}x + \frac{7}{2}$

   C. $y = \frac{3}{2}x + 2$

   D. $y = 7x - 3$

6. Given $y = ax + b$, which symbol represents the slope?

   A. y

   B. a

   C. b

   D. x

7. A computer consultant charges her client for her services based on an equation relating the total bill $f(h)$ to the number of hours worked (h). The best interpretation of the function $f(h) = 85h + 75$ is:

   A. She charges $75 per hour plus an $85 flat fee.

   B. She charges $85 per hour plus a $75 flat fee.

   C. She charges $150 per hour.

   D. Her hourly charge varies from $75 to $85 depending on the job.

8. Tom earns $10 a day from his part-time job. How much will he have after a week?

   A. $60

   B. $75

   C. $70

   D. $80

9. Use the absolute value to determine which line has a greater slope?

   One: $y = 3x + 5$

   Two: $2y + 3x = 5$

   A. One

   B. Two

   C. The lines have the same slope.

   D. It cannot be determined.

10. A company is expecting the number of employees to grow using the equation: $y = 5x + 8$, where y is the number of employees and x is the number of years after the company is established. Given the company currently has 33 employees, what is the value for x.

   A. 7 years

   B. 8 years

   C. 9 years

   D. 5 years

11. Katy collects 15 stamps a day. She started off with 42 stamps. Choose the best function to represent the number of Katy's stamps.

   A. $y = 5x + 8$

   B. $y = 42x + 15$

   C. $y = 15x + 42$

   D. $42 + y = 15x$

12. Bob collects stamps; currently he has 130 different stamps. Each year he gets 15 more stamps. Mike like to collect stamps also. Right now he has 80 different stamps and is getting 25 more each year. Who has more stamps after 14 years and by how much?

   A. Bob, by 90 stamps.

   B. Mike, by 60 stamps.

   C. Bob, by 50 stamps.

   D. Mike, by 90 stamps.

Name_____ Date _____ Class_____

Use the table for questions 13 and 14.

x	y
3	9
6	18
9	27
12	36

13. Which function rule matches the table?

   A. $y = x + 6$

   B. $y = 2x + 3$

   C. $y = 3x - 1$

   D. $y = 3x$

Gridded-Response: Fill in the grid with your answer to each question.

14. What y-value corresponds to an x-value of 7?

15. You are in charge of buying bags of pretzels and popcorn for the school picnic. A bag of pretzels costs $3.00 and a bag of popcorn costs $4. You have $48 to spend. What is the value of m in the table?

Popcorn	Pretzels
0	16
3	12
6	8
9	m
12	0

Extended-Response: Show your work for each question.

16. Write the rule for a linear function that passes through $(-3, 2)$ and has a y-intercept of 5.

17. Write the function rule for the graph below.

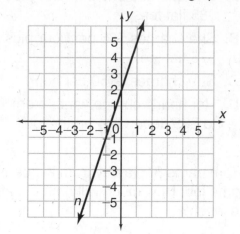

18.

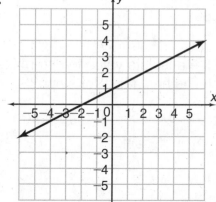

   A. If the x-intercept in the graph were to stay the same and the slope of the line decreased, what impact would that have on the y-intercept? Explain your answer.

   B. If the y-intercept in the graph were to stay the same and the x-intercept increased, what impact would that have on the slope of the line? Explain your answer.

ALGEBRA

Quadratic Functions

8.11.10 Interpret the role of the coefficients and constants on the graphs of linear and quadratic functions, given a set of equations. Also 8.11.03, III.B.8

Select the best answer for each question.

1. How is the graph for $y = x^2 + 3$ different from the graph for $y = x^2$?

   A. No difference.

   B. All y values are shifted up by 3 units.

   C. All y values are shifted down by 3 units.

   D. $y = x^2 + 3$ is a cubic function.

2. Which of the following functions is constant?

   A. $y = x$

   B. $y = 4$

   C. $y = x^3$

   D. $y = x^2$

3. Which of the following graph(s) is(are) quadratic?

   I. 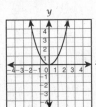 III.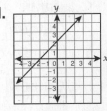

   II. 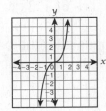 IV.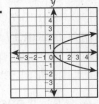

   A. I only

   B. II only

   C. I, II, and IV

   D. I and IV

4. If the equation $w = -x^2 + 6x$ models an animal's weight in x days after it is born, is it physically reasonable to discuss $w(7)$?

   A. Yes

   B. No

   C. Sometimes

   D. It cannot be determined.

5. Which of the following is a quadratic function?

A.
Input	8	6	5	4
Output	7	5	4	3

B.
Input	0	3	6	9
Output	5	15	20	25

C.
Input	2	0	-2	-4
Output	0	-2	-4	-6

D.
Input	1	0	1	2
Output	-1	0	1	4

6. The equation $h = t^2 + 6t + 8$ gives the height h of the ball from the ground and t seconds after the ball has been thrown. Is this a good model for the first few seconds?

A. Yes, it opens up.

B. No, it opens up.

C. Yes, it opens down.

D. No, it opens down.

7. If Jimmy gets $1 in day one from his mother, $4 in day two, $9 in day three, and $16 in day four, etc. what function can model this situation?

A. Quadratic only

B. Linear only

C. Cubic only

D. Both quadratic and cubic

8. If Tom has the function $y = x^2$ to represent his investment growth. Lily has $y = \frac{1}{3}x^2$ to represent her investment growth, and Tracy has the following function for her investment growth: $y = 3x^2$. Assume they all started off with the same amount of money. Who will have the highest amount of investment after 6 years?

A. Tom

B. Lily

C. Tracy

D. Lily and Tracy

9. Does the following graph belong to a quadratic function?

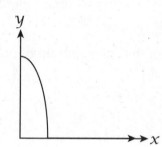

A. Yes

B. No

C. It cannot be determined.

D. None of the above

Gridded-Response: Fill in the grid with your answer to each question.

10. What is the smallest root of the quadratic equation $y = x^2 + 10x + 21$?

Extended-Response: Show your work.

11. Assume that a constant is added to the end of a quadratic function.

A. What effect does adding the constant have on the function?

B. Illustrate the effect on a coordinate graph.

MN Test Prep Grade 9

ALGEBRA

Solve Equations

8.11.16 Solve linear equations and inequalities, including selecting and evaluating formulas. Also, 8.11.22, III.B.7

Select the best answer for each question.

1. Which value of y makes the equation $36 = \dfrac{y}{2}$ true?

   A. 9
   B. 18
   C. 36
   D. 72

2. Which value of z is a solution to $3z = 9$?

   A. 3
   B. 9
   C. 27
   D. 81

3. Which equation has a solution of $x = -5$?

   A. $x - 1 = -4$
   B. $-2x = 6$
   C. $-3 - x = 2$
   D. All of the above

4. Which equation has a solution of $x = -2$?

   A. $-6x + 3 = 16$
   B. $10 - 3x = 7$
   C. $-2 - 5x = 3$
   D. $3x - 1 = -7$

5. Which value of s is the solution to this equation?

   $$17 + 4s = 53 - 3s$$

   A. -7
   B. -18
   C. 18
   D. None of the above

6. Which value of c makes the equation true?

   $$7c + 3c + 3 = 6 + 4c$$

   A. 0.5
   B. 1
   C. 2
   D. 3

MN Test Prep Grade 9

7. Which equation(s) has $x = 7$ as a solution?

Equation I

$14 - 3x = -15$

Equation II

$4x - 3 = -31$

Equation III

$16 + 5x = 51$

Equation IV

$2x - 30 = -16$

A. All of the equations

B. Equations II and III

C. Equations III and IV

D. Equations I, III and IV

8. Kelly's class is collecting box tops. Kelly has collected 60 and plans to collect an additional 5 box tops each week. The equation $y = 60 + 5x$ can be used to represent this situation. How many weeks will it take her to collect 120 box tops?

A. 8 weeks

B. 12 weeks

C. 15 weeks

D. 44 weeks

9. Allison is in charge of buying sandwiches for the music club's meeting after school. She has $48, and sandwiches cost $5.25 each. How many sandwiches can she buy?

A. 7 sandwiches

B. 8 sandwiches

C. 9 sandwiches

D. 10 sandwiches

10. Eric has 4 times as many coins as Wilma. If Eric has 116 coins, which equation would you use to find out how many coins Wilma has?

A. $c + 4 = 116$

B. $4c = 116$

C. $4(116) = c$

D. $c = \dfrac{116 + 4}{4}$

11. Donna writes an expression that will always represent an odd number. Which expression did she write, if n is an integer?

A. m^3

B. n^2

C. $n^2 + 1$

D. $2n - 1$

12. The cost of a long distance call is $2.50 for the first three minutes and $0.10 for each additional minute. Theo called home and talked for 8 minutes. Which equation would best be used to find the cost, c, for the call?

A. $\$2.50 \times 0.10 = c$

B. $\$2.50 + c = 8$

C. $\$2.50 + 0.10 = c$

D. $\$2.50 + (5 \times 0.10) = c$

13. Listed below are Shelly's scores in English class. What score does she need to earn on her last essay in order to have an average of 95% for the term?

Shelly's English Scores

Test 1	99%
Essay 1	94%
Test 2	96%
Essay 2	98%
Test 3	93%
Essay 3	?

A. 86%   C. 93%

B. 90%   D. 94%

14. Which equation has a solution of -18?

A. $3x - 9 = 45$

B. $-4 + \left(\dfrac{1}{3}\right)x = -10$

C. $\left(\dfrac{1}{6}\right)x + 3 = \left(\dfrac{1}{6}\right)(x + 3)$

D. $-x + 2 = -16$

15. Which value of y makes the equation below true?

$$105 = \dfrac{y}{6}$$

A. $y = 17.5$

B. $y = 600$

C. $y = 630$

D. $y = 660$

Gridded-Response: Fill in the grid with your answer to each question.

16. Mitchell is paid twice the normal hourly wage for each hour he works over 40 hours in a week. Last week he worked 50 hours and earned $754.20. What is Mitchell's hourly wage?

17. At the circus, an adult ticket costs 3 times more than a child's ticket. 2 adults and 3 children tickets cost $45.00. What is the cost of an adult ticket to the circus?

18. Ava's hourly wage is $9, and she earns at least $2 more per hour than Kevin. Write and solve an inequality to represent the possible values of Kevin's hourly wage. Graph the solution on a number line. Suppose Kevin got a raise of $0.50 per hour. Explain the difference in the graph of the solution of the inequality.

MN Test Prep Grade 9

ALGEBRA

Solve Inequalitites

8.11.16 Solve linear equations and inequalities, including selecting and evaluating formulas. Also Also, 8.11.22, III.B.7

Select the best answer for each question.

1. Which inequality represents the phrase, "5 is greater than a number increased by 3 and then multiplied by 2"?

   A. $5 > x + (3)(2)$
   B. $5 < x + (3)(2)$
   C. $2(x + 3) > 5$
   D. $2(x + 3) < 5$

2. Solve the following inequality.

   $$6(x - 2) > 18$$

   A. $x > 5$
   B. $x < 5$
   C. $x > -5$
   D. $x < -5$

3. Solve the following inequality.

   $$-2(x + 2) < -2x + 4$$

   A. $x > 2$
   B. $x < 2$
   C. $x > -2$
   D. None of the above

4. Describe the solution of $3x \le 21$.

   A. All real numbers less than 7
   B. All real numbers less than or equal to 7
   C. All real numbers greater than or equal to 7
   D. All real numbers less than 18

5. Which of the following linear inequalities has the solution $x > 1$?

   A. $4x + 8 > 4$
   B. $4x + 12 < 8$
   C. $6 - 3x > 3$
   D. None of the above

6. Which inequality is equivalent to $x \le -4$?

   A. $x \ge \dfrac{1}{4}$
   B. $-x \le -4$
   C. $-x \ge 4$
   D. $-x \le \dfrac{1}{4}$

 MN Test Prep Grade 9

7. The maximum grade on a test is 85. The minimum grade is 60. If n represents a grade, which sentence best expresses this situation?

A. $85 = n = 60$

B. $85 \geq n \geq 60$

C. $60 \leq n \geq 85$

D. $85 \geq n \geq 60$

8. A recipe for cake calls for 150–250 mL of water. If w represents the amount of water to be put in the cake, which of the following inequalities is correct?

A. $150 < w < 250$

B. $150 \leq w \leq 250$

C. $150 > w > 250$

D. $150 \geq w \geq 250$

9. Three times a number, then decreased by 5 is less than 4. What are the possible values for the number?

A. The number is less than 3.

B. The number is less than −3.

C. The number is greater than 3.

D. The number is greater than −3.

10. John took a test that had 50 questions worth one point each. He didn't answer 5 of the questions, and he knows he answered 30 correctly for sure. Which inequality represents the range of his percentage grade on the test?

A. $60 < g < 90$ **C.** $30 < g < 45$

B. $60 \leq g \leq 90$ **D.** $30 \leq g \leq 45$

11. The number line below represents the solution to which equation?

A. $|w| = -1$ **C.** $|w| = 5$

B. $|w + 3| = 2$ **D.** $|w + 7| = 2$

12. Colton has $20. He wants to buy as many tickets for a draw as he can. Each ticket costs $0.75. Which inequality would you use to find out how many tickets, n, Colton can buy?

A. $20 \leq 0.75n$

B. $20 \leq 0.75 + n$

C. $20 - n \leq 0.75$

D. $20 \geq 0.75n$

13. Alexis earns $6.75 per hour babysitting. She needs at least $25 to go on a field trip. Which inequality would you use to find out how many hours, h, Alexis needs to babysit?

A. $6.75h > 25$

B. $6.75h \leq 25$

C. $6.75h \geq 25$

D. $6.75h < 25$

14. Martin is going to make a rectangle with a 36-inch perimeter by bending a 36-inch long wire. The length of the rectangle must exceed 10 inches. Let w be the width of the rectangle. Which inequality expresses the possible values of w?

A. $0 < w < 8$

B. $0 < w \leq 8$

C. $0 < w < 16$

D. $0 < w \leq 16$

15. Hannah made 20 goodie bags for a party. Each bag contains 150 to 200 jelly beans. Which inequality gives the best possible limits on the total number t of jelly beans in all 20 goodie bags?

A. $150 \leq t \leq 200$

B. $1500 \leq t \leq 2000$

C. $3000 \leq t \leq 4000$

D. $5000 \leq t \leq 10{,}000$

16. Which linear inequality is equivalent to $-5x + 2 > 7$?

A. $x < -1$

B. $x > -1$

C. $x < 1$

D. $x > 1$

Gridded-Response: Fill in the grid with your answer to each question.

17. An elevator has a maximum capacity of 2000 lbs. Five passengers total 888 pounds. What is the most additional weight the elevator can safely carry?

Extended-Response: Show your work.

18. Elizabeth earned scores of 77, 85, 80, and 92 on her past 4 math tests. In order to earn a B in the class, Elizabeth needs an 82 average.

A. Write an inequality that describes the possible scores Elizabeth can earn on her next math test in order to achieve an overall B average.

B. Can Elizabeth achieve an average of 90? Explain your answer.

MN Test Prep Grade 9

ALGEBRA

Systems of Equations and Inequalities

8.11.17 Solve systems of equations and inequalitites. Also 8.11.15 and 8.11.22 III.B.11

Select the best answer for each question.

1. Which ordered pair represents the solution to the following linear system?

   $y = 4x - 4$

   $y = -2x + 8$

   A. $(4, 2)$
   B. $(-4, -2)$
   C. $(2, 4)$
   D. $(2, -4)$

2. What are the coordinates of the solution to this linear system?

   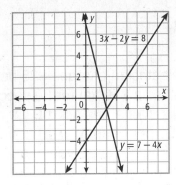

   A. $(2, 1)$
   B. $(-2, 1)$
   C. $(-1, 2)$
   D. $(2, -1)$

3. In which case would a system of linear equations have no solutions?

   A. The lines are perpendicular.
   B. The lines are parallel.
   C. The lines have the same equation.
   D. A, B, and C are all correct.

4. Which ordered pair represents the solution to the following linear system?

   $3y + 6x = 12$

   $6y + 10x = 18$

   A. $(-3, -2)$
   B. $(2, 3)$
   C. $(2, -3)$
   D. $(3, -2)$

5. Which of the following linear systems has the solution $(4, 5)$?

   A. $y = 3x - 7$
      $y = 4x + 3$

   B. $y = 3x - 7$
      $2y - x = 3$

   C. $y = 3x + 1$
      $2y - 5x = 32$

   D. $2y = 3x - 2$
      $y - x = 1$

6. Which graph represents the solution of the inequality $4x + 1 < 17$ or $3x - 11 \geq 10$?

A.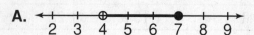

B.

C.

D.

7. A book club offers two membership plans. The first plan costs $25 per month. The second plan costs $18 per month plus $2 for each visit to the club. Which is the least number of visits you need to make so the first plan is worthwhile?

A. 2

B. 3

C. 4

D. 5

8. Five footballs and 3 hockey sticks cost $69. The cost of 3 footballs and 6 hockey sticks is $96. Which system of equations could be used to find the costs of one football and of one hockey stick?

A. $5f + 3h = 69$
$3f + 6h = 96$

B. $3f + 6h = 69$
$5f + 3h = 96$

C. $3f + 5h = 69$
$6f + 3h = 96$

D. $6f + 3h = 69$
$3f + 5h = 96$

9. Referring to question 8, how much does one hockey stick cost?

A. $6

B. $13

C. $23

D. $34

10. One electrician charges $25 per hour, as well as a $50 flat fee. A second electrician charges a $100 flat fee, and $20 per hour. At what hour would the two amounts be equal, and which electrician would be cheaper for any hours after that?

A. 5, first

B. 10, first

C. 20, it would be the same

D. 10, second

11. Choose the statement that is true for a system of two linear equations.

   A. A system can only be solved by graphing the equations.

   B. There are infinitely many solutions when the graphs of the equations have the same slope and intercepts.

   C. There is exactly one solution when the graphs of the equations are one line.

   D. When solving a system by substitution the first step is to add the equations.

12. A farmer raises apples and peaches on 215 acres of land. If he wants to plant 31 more acres in apples than peaches, which system of equations will help determine how many acres of each he should plant?

   A. $a + p = 215$
       $a + p = 31$

   B. $a - p = 215$
       $a + p = 31$

   C. $a + p = 215$
       $a - p = 31$

   D. $a - p = 215$
       $a - p = 31$

13. To solve the following system of equations by elimination, which step would you perform first?

$$10a + 6b = 8$$
$$5a + 3b = 2$$

   A. Add the two equations.

   B. Subtract the two equations.

   C. Multiply both equations by -2.

   D. Multiply equation 2 by -2.

Gridded-Response: Fill in the grid with your answer to each question.

14. What is the value of x in the system of equations?
$$5x = 4y - 7$$
$$8y = 6x + 2$$

15. Which is the x-coordinate of the ordered pair solving the system $\begin{array}{l} 2x + y = -5 \\ 3x + 5y = -4 \end{array}$?

Extended-Response: Show your work for each question.

16. Your chemistry teacher is preparing lab samples. He has 30% and 80% alcohol solutions. He needs 100 mL of a 50% alcohol solution. How many milliliters of the 30% solution should he mix with the 80% solution?

17. The perimeter of a rectangle is 54 in. The length is 3 in. more than the width. What is the length of the rectangle?

18. Megan has $6,000 to invest. She earns $350 in interest by putting part of it in her savings account that pays 3% interest and the remainder in stocks that yield 8%. Write a system of equations that can be used to determine how much she invests at each rate.

19. Solve the system. Explain your answer.

$$2a - 3b = -6$$
$$2(a + 4) = 3b$$

20. Solve the system. Explain your answer.

$$5x + 3y = 21$$
$$\frac{x + 5}{4} = y$$

21. The slope-intercept form of a line is $y = mx + b$.

   A. Explain how you could use the slope-intercept form to write a system of equations to find the equation of the line through (1, 3) and (5, 5).

   B. Explain how you could use the method from part A to write a formula for the equation of the line through the points (x_1, y_1) and (x_2, y_2).

GEOMETRY
Triangles

9.G1.3 Find and use measures of sides and interior and exterior angles of triangles and polygons to classify figures (e.g., scalene, isosceles, and equilateral triangles; rectangles [square and non-square]; other convex polygons). Also 9.G3.2, V.B.3

Select the best answer for each question.

1. A triangle has side lengths of 5, 5, and 7 units. What kind of triangle is it?

   A. equilateral
   B. isosceles
   C. right
   D. scalene

2. Two of the angles in a triangle measure 70° and 40°. What kind of triangle is it?

   A. equilateral
   B. isosceles
   C. right
   D. scalene

3. Two of the angles in a triangle measure 50° and 70°. What kind of triangle is it?

   A. equilateral
   B. isosceles
   C. right
   D. scalene

4. If the sides of a triangle all have the same length, what kind of triangle is it?

   A. equilateral
   B. isosceles
   C. right
   D. scalene

5. Triangle A is dilated by a scale factor of 2 to produce triangle B. How are the two triangles related?

   A. They are congruent.
   B. They are similar.
   C. They are reflections of each other.
   D. There is not enough information to determine the relationship.

6. One of the angles in an isosceles triangle is 100°. What are the measures of the remaining two angles?

   A. 40° and 40°
   B. 40° and 60°
   C. 20° and 80°
   D. 20° and 100°

7. If the height of a triangle is doubled, but its base remains fixed, how does its area change?

   A. It remains fixed.
   B. It halves.
   C. It doubles.
   D. It depends on the exact length of the base.

8. A triangle is modified by reducing its height by a third and enlarging its base. How much must the base be enlarged if the area remains unchanged?

A. The base must be increased by 50%.

B. The base must be doubled in length.

C. The base must be tripled in length.

D. The base must be quadrupled in length.

9. Which set of interior angle measures listed below can be angles of a scalene triangle?

A. 30°, 30°, 120°

B. 25°, 45°, 100°

C. 45°, 150°, 10°

D. 35°, 70°, 75°

10. A triangle has 3 sides of different lengths. Classify the triangle.

A. equilateral

B. isosceles

C. right

D. scalene

11. A triangle has an exterior angle of 95°. Which of the following is not a possible classification for this triangle?

A. equilateral

B. isosceles

C. right

D. scalene

Gridded-Response: Fill in the grid with your answer to each question.

12. A triangle is dilated by a factor of 5. How many times larger in area is the dilated triangle compared to the original?

Extended-Response: Show your work.

13. Draw an example of each triangle, or explain why it does not exist.

A. scalene triangle *ABC* with a right angle at vertex *A* and an obtuse angle at vertex *C*

B. right isosceles triangle *DEF* with a right angle at vertex *D* and side $\overline{DE}$ congruent to side $\overline{DF}$

C. isosceles triangle *GHJ* with a 50° angle at vertex *G* and a 60° angle at vertex *H*

GEOMETRY

Three-Dimensional Figures

9.11.06 Identify a three-dimensional object from different perspectives. V.B.3

Select the best answer for each question.

1. Which figure(s) are nets for a cube?

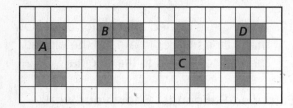

   A. Figures *A* and *D*
   B. Figures *C* and *D*
   C. Figures *A*, *B*, and *C*
   D. All of the above

2. This figure is the net for an object. What is the object?

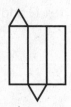

   A. Triangular pyramid
   B. Rectangular pyramid
   C. Triangular prism
   D. Rectangular prism

3. A solid has 4 congruent rectangular faces and 2 congruent square faces. What is the solid?

   A. Triangular pyramid
   B. Rectangular pyramid
   C. Triangular prism
   D. Rectangular prism

4. What is a similarity between a cylinder and a cone?

   A. Number of vertexes
   B. Number of faces
   C. Shape of the bases
   D. Number of right angles

5. Which of the following statements is always true?

   A. A triangular prism always has equilateral triangle as its base.
   B. A rectangular prism has only right angles.
   C. A cone has no vertex.
   D. A cylinder has no congruent faces.

 MN Test Prep Grade 9

6. This figure shows the front-right view of an object made of cubes.

Which figure shows the left view?

A.

B.

C.

D.

7. The base of a prism is a polygon with N sides. Which expression equals the number of faces in this prism?

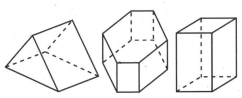

A. $2 + N$
B. $2 \cdot (N + 1)$
C. $2 \cdot N$
D. $2 \cdot (N - 1)$

8. Which of the following solids have the most pairs of congruent faces?

A. Cylinder
B. Rectangular prism
C. Sphere
D. Tetrahedron

9. Which of the following statements is FALSE?

A. A pyramid always has parallel faces.
B. A prism always has parallel faces.
C. A prism never has perpendicular faces.
D. Both A and D are false.

10. From which three-dimensional figure can you obtain a triangular cross-section?

A. A pyramid
B. A cone
C. A triangular prism
D. All of the above

11. Mary observes that the solid she is studying has 2 triangular faces that are the same and 3 different rectangular faces. Which solid is she studying?

   A. rectangular prism

   B. tetrahedron

   C. triangular prism

   D. pyramid

12. Janet claims that she can find the surface area and volume of a specific solid given only one side length. For which of the following solids would that be true?

   A. cube

   B. square pyramid

   C. rectangular prism

   D. cone

13. The globe that you just bought shows a line at the equator. What shape best describes the equator?

   A. line segment

   B. ray

   C. circle

   D. square

14. You are making a model and need to cut a long, thin dowel in half along its length. What is the shape of the cross-section?

   length

   A. rectangle

   B. circle

   C. triangle

   D. semicircle

15. How many lateral faces doea a cylinder have?

   A. circle

   B. triangle

   C. rectangle

   D. trapezoid

Extended-Response: Show your work.

16. The following silo consists of a cylinder with a hemisphere on top. Use π = 3.14.

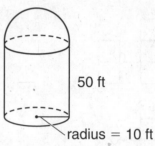

   50 ft

   radius = 10 ft

   A. Explain how you would find the volume of the silo.

   B. Suppose the radius of the silo were doubled. What would the effect be on the volume of the silo?

44

GEOMETRY

Coordinate Geometry

9.11.09 Solve problems that involve calculating distance, midpoint, and slope using coordinate geometry. Also 8.11.20, 9.11.16 V.B.5

Select the best answer for each question.

1. Which line on the graph has a negative slope?

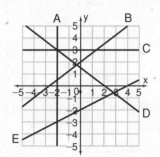

A. A   **C.** C

B. B   **D.** D

2. The line shown contains the points (−2, 4) and (2, −2). What is the slope of the line?

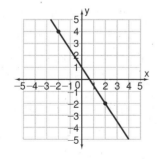

A. $-\dfrac{3}{2}$ **C.** $\dfrac{2}{3}$

B. $-\dfrac{2}{3}$ **D.** $\dfrac{3}{2}$

3. What is the equation of the line?

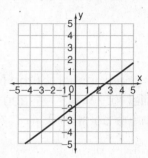

A. $y = 3x + 4$

B. $y = x - 2$

C. $y = \dfrac{3}{4}x + 2$

D. $y = \dfrac{3}{4}x - 2$

Use the graph for questions 4 and 5.

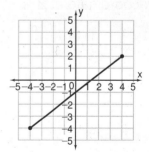

4. What is the distance between points *A* and *B*?

A. 2   **C.** 8

B. 4   **D.** 10

5. What is the midpoint of $\overline{AB}$?

A. (0, −1)   **C.** (−2, 2)

B. (−1, 0)   **D.** (0, −2)

45 **MN Test Prep Grade 9**

6. What is the slope of the line perpendicular to the line $y = \frac{1}{2}x + 6$?

A. -2

B. $-\frac{1}{2}$

C. $\frac{1}{6}$

D. $\frac{1}{2}$

7. What is the equation of the line that is parallel to $y = 4x + 1$ and passes through the point $(-3, 4)$?

A. $y = 4x - 8$

B. $y = 4x - 7$

C. $y = 4x + 1$

D. $y = 4x + 16$

8. The center of C is $(0, 2)$. Point $W(-6, -4)$ lies on the circle. If $\overline{WZ}$ is a diameter of the circle, what is the x-coordinate of Z?

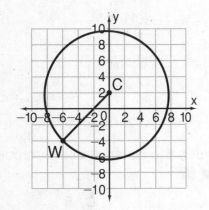

A. 2

B. 0

C. 4

D. 6

Use the diagram for questions 9 and 10.

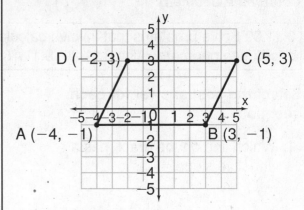

9. What is the equation of the line containing $\overline{AB}$?

A. $y = -1$

B. $x = -1$

C. $2x + 7y = 1$

D. $x + 7y = 15$

10. Find the equation of the line of $\overline{CB}$ in standard form.

A. $y = -1$

B. $x = -1$

C. $y = 2x - 7$

D. $y = 2x - 13$

MN Test Prep Grade 9

11. Which quadrant has the most points?

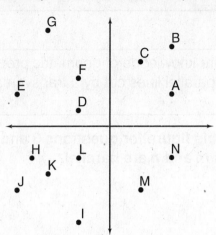

A. I

B. II

C. III

D. IV

Use the coordinate grid shown below for questions 12–14.

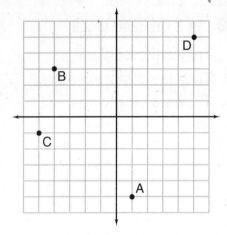

12. For which points is $x < 0$?

A. A and B

B. A and C

C. B and C

D. A and B

13. Which point's *y*-coordinate is less than −4?

14. Which point is represented by the ordered pair (5, 5)?

Extended-Response: Show your work.

15. Triangle *ABC* has vertices $A(-3, -2)$, $B(1, -2)$, and $C(-3, 4)$.

A. Draw triangle *ABC* and classify it by its sides and angles. Explain your answer.

B. Compare the lengths of the sides of triangle *ABC*. Identify the longest side and shortest side. Explain your answer.

GEOMETRY

Parallel Lines

9.11.05 Identify, apply, or solve problems that require knowledge of geometric properties of plane figures (e.g., triangles, quadrilaterals, parallel lines cut by a transversal,
angles, diagonals, triangle inequality). V.B.1

**Select the best answer for each
question.**

**Use this figure for questions 1 and 2.
Lines *g* and *h* are parallel.**

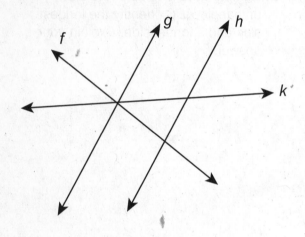

1. Which lines are transversals for
parallel lines *g* and *h*?

A. Line *f*

B. Line *k*

C. Lines *f* and *k*

D. Lines *f*, *g*, and *k*

2. Which lines intersect in a common
point?

A. Lines *f*, *g*, and *h*

B. Lines *f*, *g*, and *k*

C. Lines *f*, *h*, and *k*

D. Lines *g*, *h*, and *k*

**Use this figure for questions 3 and 4.
Lines *m* and *n* are parallel.**

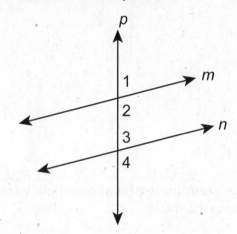

3. How is ∠1 related to ∠2?

A. They are congruent.

B. They are complementary.

C. They are supplementary.

D. They are obtuse.

4. Which angle corresponds with ∠2?

A. ∠1

B. ∠3

C. ∠4

D. All of the above correspond with ∠2.

5. Line *a* is parallel to line *b*. Line *b* is
perpendicular to line *c*. How are lines
a and *c* related?

A. The lines are parallel.

B. The lines are perpendicular.

C. The lines intersect, but are not
perpendicular.

D. The lines are reflections.

48

Use this figure for questions 6–9. Two of the lines are parallel.

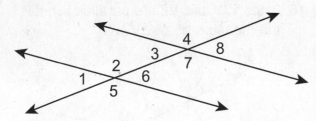

6. Which is a pair of congruent vertical angles?

    A. $\angle 1$ and $\angle 3$

    B. $\angle 1$ and $\angle 4$

    C. $\angle 1$ and $\angle 5$

    D. $\angle 1$ and $\angle 6$

7. Which are the interior angles?

    A. $\angle 1$, $\angle 2$, $\angle 5$, and $\angle 6$

    B. $\angle 2$, $\angle 3$, $\angle 5$, and $\angle 8$

    C. $\angle 2$, $\angle 4$, $\angle 6$, and $\angle 8$

    D. $\angle 2$, $\angle 3$, $\angle 6$, and $\angle 7$

8. If $m\angle 6 = 40°$, what is $m\angle 3$?

    A. $20°$

    B. $40°$

    C. $50°$

    D. $80°$

9. Which pair of angles is NOT congruent?

    A. $\angle 1$ and $\angle 2$

    B. $\angle 1$ and $\angle 3$

    C. $\angle 2$ and $\angle 5$

    D. $\angle 1$ and $\angle 6$

10. Which of the following is an equation of a line that is parallel to the graph of the equation $5x - 10y = 8$?

    A. $x + 2y = 21$

    B. $2x + y = 24$

    C. $5x + 10y = 12$

    D. $-x + 2y = 20$

11. The equations $y = x - 3$ and $y = x + 4$ are graphed on the same set of axes. Which of the following statements is true?

    A. The lines are perpendicular.

    B. The lines are parallel.

    C. The lines intersect on the x-axis.

    D. The lines intersect on the y-axis.

12. Lines L_1 and L_2 are parallel. If the slope of $L_1 = \frac{3}{4}$, what is the slope of L_2?

    A. $\frac{4}{3}$ **C.** $\frac{3}{4}$

    B. $-\frac{3}{4}$ **D.** $-\frac{4}{3}$

13 Which of the following statements is true?

    A. $y = 3x - 1$ and $3x - y = 2$ are parallel.

    B. $y = 2x + 5$ and $2x + y = 5$ are parallel lines.

    C. $5x - 3y = 9$ and $6x + 10y = 12$ are parallel lines.

    D. $y = \frac{2}{3}x + 2$ and $4x + 6y = 4$ are parallel lines.

14. Which of the following pairs of linear equations are parallel lines?

A. $y = \frac{3}{4}x - 2$

$3x - 4y = 2$

B. $2x - 5y = 3$

$5x - 2y = 4$

C. $3x - y = 10$

$x + 3y = 10$

D. $2x - 5y = 10$

$2x - 10y = 20$

15. Which of the following systems of equations are parallel lines?

A. $y = \frac{2}{3}x - 5$

$3x - 2y = 4$

B. $5x - 6y = 11$

$2x - 3y = 8$

C. $6x + 5y = 12$

$5x - 6y = 8$

D. $2x + 3y = 8$

$y = -\frac{2}{3}x + 12$

Gridded-Response: Fill in the grid with your answer to each question.

16. Lines $\overline{WY}$ and $\overline{VZ}$ are parallel. What is the measure of $\angle YZV$?

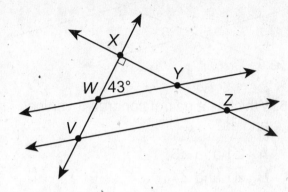

Extended-Response: Show your work.

17. Lines m and n are both parallel to $y = -2x + 7$.

A. Use slopes to explain why lines m and n must be parallel to each other.

B. Suppose that line m passes through the point $(3, 1)$. Explain how you would find the equation of line m.

GEOMETRY

Transformations

9.11.02 Identify and represent transformations (rotations, reflections, translations, dilations) of an object in the plane, and describe the effects of transformations on points in words or coordinates. V.B.6

Select the best answer for each question.

1. Which of the following terms is not a term representing a transformation?

   A. Reflection   **C.** Translation

   B. Dilation   **D.** Transportation

2. How many lines of symmetry does the figure have?

   A. 0   **C.** 2

   B. 1   **D.** 3

3. What is the transformation from Figure 1 to Figure 2?

Figure 1   Figure 2

   A. Translation

   B. Reflection

   C. Rotation

   D. Translation, translation

4. What is the transformation from Figure 1 to Figure 2?

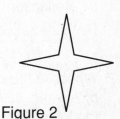

Figure 1   Figure 2

   A. Translation

   B. Reflection

   C. Rotation

   D. Translation, translation

5. What is the transformation from Figure 1 to Figure 2?

Figure 1   Figure 2

   A. Translation

   B. Reflection

   C. Rotation

   D. Translation, translation

51

6. Which type of transformation is shown below?

A. Translation

B. Rotation

C. Reflection

D. Glide reflection

7. What are the coordinates of the image of A when ABC is translated 6 units to the left?

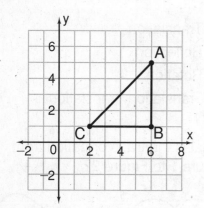

A. (0, 5)

B. (0, −1)

C. (12, 5)

D. (12, −1)

8. What is the image of point (4, −6) when it is reflected across the x-axis?

A. (−4, 6)

B. (−4, −6)

C. (−6, 4)

D. (4, 6)

9. Which transformation reverses orientation?

A. Translation

B. Rotation

C. Reflection

D. Slide

10. The solid colored figure represents the preimage of a dilation, and the outlined figure represents the image. What is the scale factor?

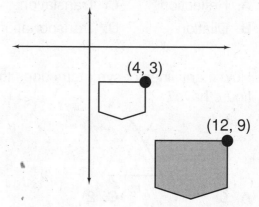

A. $\frac{1}{2}$

B. $\frac{1}{3}$

C. 2

D. 3

MN Test Prep Grade 9

11. Identify the transformation from Figure A to Figure B.

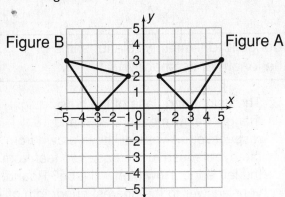

Figure B   Figure A

A. translation

B. reflection

C. rotation

D. translation, reflection

Use the figure to answer questions 12 and 13.

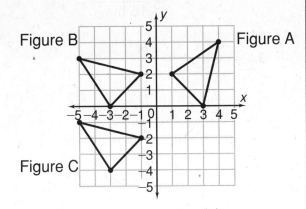

Figure B   Figure A

Figure C

12. Identify the transformation from Figure A to Figure C.

A. translation

B. reflection

C. translation, reflection

D. rotation, translation

13. Identify the transformation from Figure B to Figure A.

A. translation

B. reflection

C. rotation

D. dilation

Gridded-Response: Fill in the grid with your answer to each question.

14. How many lines of symmetry does an equilateral triangle have?

Extended-Response: Show your work.

15.

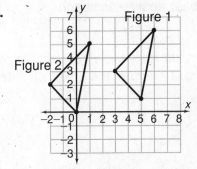

Figure 2   Figure 1

A. Compare the rule to transform figure 1 to figure 2 with the rule to transform figure 2 to figure 1.

B. Graph the reflection of figure 1 across the x-axis. Explain the rule for the transformation in terms of the x- and y-coordinates of the vertices.

MN Test Prep Grade 9

GEOMETRY

Similar Triangles

9.G4.1 Solve real-world problems using congruence and similarity relationships of triangles (e.g., find the height of a pole given the length of its shadow).

Select the best answer for each question.

1. The right triangles shown are similar. What is the length of the unknown side?

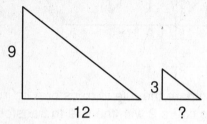

A. $\frac{9}{4}$

B. 4

C. 5

D. 6

2. The triangles are similar. What is the length of the unknown side?

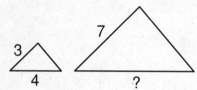

A. $\frac{7}{12}$

B. $1\frac{5}{7}$

C. $5\frac{1}{4}$

D. $9\frac{1}{3}$

3. The height and base of the outside right triangle below measure 28 ft and 18 ft respectively. A vertical line is drawn from the hypotenuse to the base two feet from the left edge. How high will it be? Round your answer to the nearest hundredth of a foot.

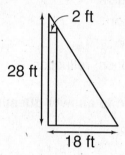

A. 23.11 ft

B. 24.00 ft

C. 24.89 ft

D. 25.32ft

4. The two triangles are similar. What is the measure of the unknown side? Round your answer to the nearest hundredth.

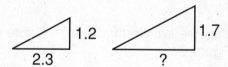

A. 0.89

B. 1.62

C. 2.80

D. 3.26

5. Angle A is congruent to $\angle B$ and supplementary to $\angle C$. If $m\angle B = 30°$, what is $m\angle C$?

A. 150°   C. 30°

B. 90°   D. 80°

54

In the figure below, segments *AX*, *BY*, and *CZ* are parallel. Segments *AB*, *BC*, and *CO* are congruent. Use the figure for questions 6–8.

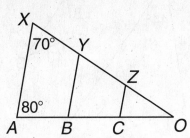

6. What is m∠*CZO*?

   A. 10°

   B. 30°

   C. 70°

   D. 80°

7. If *CZ* is 6 centimeters, what is *AX*?

   A. 2 cm

   B. 4 cm

   C. 12 cm

   D. 18 cm

8. If *XZ* is 20 inches, what is *YO*?

   A. 10 in.

   B. 20 in.

   C. 30 in.

   D. 40 in.

Use these similar triangles for questions 9 and 10.

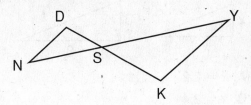

9. Which of the following is a proportion that shows the relationships among two of the corresponding sides?

   A. $\dfrac{NS}{YS} = \dfrac{DS}{YK}$

   B. $\dfrac{DS}{KS} = \dfrac{ND}{NY}$

   C. $\dfrac{ND}{YK} = \dfrac{NS}{YS}$

   D. $\dfrac{ND}{YK} = \dfrac{NS}{NY}$

10. If m∠*SKY* = 110°, what does m∠*NDS* measure?

   A. 60°

   B. 70°

   C. 80°

   D. 110°

Name_____ Date _____ Class_____

11. Find the value of x that makes the two right triangles similar.

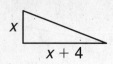

x + 4

3

8

A. x = 2.2

B. x = 2.4

C. x = 2.8

D. x = 6.4

12. What value of x will make these two isosceles triangles similar?

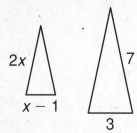

2x

x − 1

7

3

A. $x = \frac{7}{9}$

B. $x = 1\frac{2}{9}$

C. x = 2

D. x = 7

Gridded-Response: Fill in the grid with your answer to each question.

13. A model builder wants to model a right triangular lot that has legs of 135 feet and 75 feet. The model is to have its longer leg 4 inches longer than the shorter leg. Find the dimensions of the shorter leg.

Triangle *ABC* is similar to triangle *DEF*.

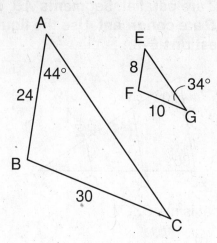

A

44°

24

B

30

C

E

8

F

34°

10

G

14. What is the scale factor?

Extended-Response: Show your work.

15.

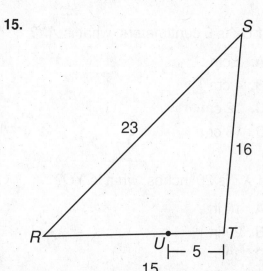

S

23

16

R

U ⊢ 5 ⊣ T

15

A. In triangle *RST*, where should point *V* be located on side $\overline{ST}$ so that triangle *UVT* is similar to triangle *RST*? Explain your answer.

B. Suppose the area of triangle *RST* is 105 square units. Explain how you would find the area of triangle *UVT*.

56

GEOMETRY

Pythagorean Theorem

9.11.01 Apply the Pythagorean theorem. V.B.3

Select the best answer for each question.

1. In the right triangle shown, find the length of the unknown side.

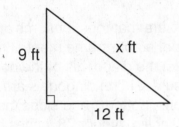

9 ft x ft

12 ft

A. $\sqrt{21}$ feet

B. 15 feet

C. 21 feet

D. 54 feet

2. In the right triangle shown, find the length of the unknown side.

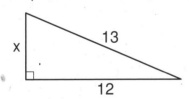

13

x

12

A. 1

B. 5

C. 25

D. 19.69

3. A light pole is 24 feet high. It is to be stabilized with a guy wire stretched from the top of the pole to a position seven feet from the base of the pole. How long must the guy wire be to stabilize the pole?

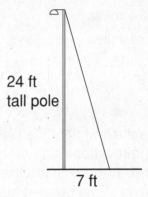

24 ft tall pole

7 ft

A. 17 feet

B. 25 feet

C. 27 feet

D. 31 feet

4. A police officer goes out on a call. He leaves the station and drives 9 miles east, then makes a right turn and drives 21 miles south. How far is the officer from the station? Approximate the answer and round to the nearest hundredth.

A. 18.45 miles

B. 18.46 miles

C. 21.93 miles

D. 22.85 miles

5. Reba has found that her cell phone will operate if it is no more than seventeen miles from a cell phone tower. If Reba lives eight miles north of the nearest tower, how far west is she able to drive and still operate her cell phone using that tower?

A. $2\sqrt{34}$ miles

B. $3\sqrt{14}$ miles

C. 15 miles

D. $\sqrt{353}$ miles

6. What is the length of the diagonal of a square whose side measures 20 inches? Approximate the answer and round to the nearest hundredth.

A. 27.12 in.

B. 28.28 in.

C. 29.17 in.

D. 30.00 in.

7. Which of the following are measures of three sides of a right triangle?

A. 1, 2, 3

B. 4, 7, 8

C. 3, 7, 9

D. 9, 12, 15

8. Suppose you are making a sail in the shape of a right triangle. The length of the longest side is 65 feet. The sail is to be 63 feet high. What is the length of the third side of the sail?

A. 2 feet

B. 15 feet

C. 16 feet

D. 20 feet

9. To ensure that tops, bottoms and sides of a door frame meet at right angles, the diagonals of the door are measured. If the diagonals are equal, the tops, bottoms and sides meet at right angles. A door 78 inches high has diagonals that are equal and are 84.5 inches long. How wide is the door? Approximate the answer and round to the nearest hundredth.

A. 13.5 inches

B. 32.50 inches

C. 55.15 inches

D. 65.91 inches

MN Test Prep Grade 9

10. Reba has found that her cell phone will operate if it is no more than 17 miles from a cell phone tower. If Reba lives 8 miles north of the nearest tower, how far west is she able to drive and still operate her cell phone using that tower?

    17 mi   8 mi

  A. $2\sqrt{34}$ mi
  B. $3\sqrt{14}$ mi
  C. 15 mi
  D. $\sqrt{353}$ mi

11. Which of the following are measures of three sides of a right triangle?

  A. 4, 7, 8   C. 10, 15, 20
  B. 3, 7, 9   D. 9, 12, 15

Gridded-Response: Fill in the grid with your answer to each question.

12. What is the length of the diagonal of a square whose side measures 20 inches? Approximate the answer and round to the nearest hundredth.

Extended-Response: Show your work for each question.

13. Suppose you are making a sail in the shape of a right triangle. The length of the longest side is 65 feet. The sail is to be 63 feet high. What is the length of the third side of the sail?

14. To ensure that tops, bottoms and sides of a door frame meet at right angles, the diagonals of the door are measured. If the diagonals are equal, the tops, bottoms and sides meet at right angles. A door 78 inches high has diagonals that are equal and are 84.5 inches long. How wide is the door? Approximate the answer and round to the nearest hundredth.

15. Max's school has a rectangular courtyard that measures 96 meters by 72 meters. How much shorter is the walk from the library to the school along the diagonal sidewalk than through point A?

Library

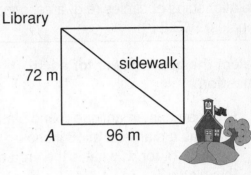

72 m   sidewalk

A   96 m

16. In the diagram below, find the distance z.

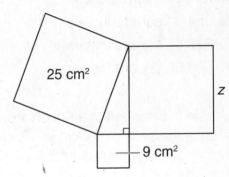

25 cm^2 z

9 cm^2

Explain how you found your answer.

17. A cat is stuck 35 feet up a tree. A firefighter sits his ladder 8 feet away from the tree to reach it.

  A. How long is the ladder? (Round to the nearest foot.) Explain your answer.

  B. If the cat climbs up another 5 feet, will the firefighter still be able to reach the cat if he moves his ladder closer to the tree? Explain your answer.

GEOMETRY

Circles

9.11.10 Identify, apply, and solve problems that require knowledge of geometric relationships of circles (e.g. arcs, chords, tangents, secants, central angles, inscribed angles). V.B.2

Select the best answer for each question.

1. Brennan has an antique round platter that has a diameter of 18 inches. Using 3.14 for π, what is the area of this platter?

   A. 56.52 square inches

   B. 254.34 square inches

   C. 313.56 square inches

   D. 508.68 square inches

2. A circle is inscribed in a 9-inch square. What is the area of the circle? Round your answer to the nearest hundredth. Use 3.14 for π.

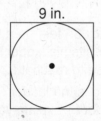
9 in.

   A. 63.59 square inches

   B. 81 square inches.

   C. 254.34 square inches

   D. 1,017.36 square inches

3. Rebecca has a bicycle with tires 24 inches in diameter, and Samuel has a bicycle with tires 36 inches in diameter. How much larger is the circumference of Samuel's tires than the circumference of Rebecca's tires?

   A. 12 inches   **C.** 58.31 inches

   B. 37.68 inches   **D.** 75.36 inches

4. A frame 3 inches wide surrounds a circular mirror. What is the outside circumference of the mirror and frame? Use 3.14 for π.

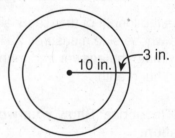
10 in.   3 in.

   A. 28.67 inches   **C.** 62.80 inches

   B. 40.82 inches   **D.** 81.64 inches

5. The top of a table is a semicircle. The straight part of the table is 40 inches long. What is the area of the top of the table? Use 3.14 for π.

   A. 62.8 square inches

   B. 314 square inches

   C. 628 square inches

   D. 1256 square inches

60

Use this figure for questions 6 and 7.

6. Name the secant of this circle.

   A. $\overleftrightarrow{AK}$

   B. $\overleftrightarrow{CD}$

   C. $\overleftrightarrow{FG}$

   D. $\overleftrightarrow{HJ}$

7. Name the tangent of this circle.

   A. $\overleftrightarrow{AB}$

   B. $\overleftrightarrow{CE}$

   C. $\overleftrightarrow{FG}$

   D. $\overleftrightarrow{HJ}$

8. Which statement is TRUE?

   A. A tangent to a circle intersects the circle at two points.

   B. A chord is a radius of a circle.

   C. A secant is a line that intersects a circle at two points.

   D. A radius is equal to 2 diameters.

9. How is the hypotenuse of $\triangle ABC$ related to circle P?

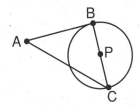

   A. It is the diameter of the circle.

   B. It contains a chord of the circle.

   C. It divides the circle into two halves.

   D. It is a radius of the circle.

10. Choose the best description of this figure.

   A. Three small semicircles have been drawn inside a larger circle.

   B. The radius of each small semicircle is $\frac{1}{3}$ as long as the radius of the large semicircle.

   C. The diameter of each small semicircle is $\frac{1}{3}$ as long as the diameter of the large semicircle.

   D. Both H and I are correct.

Gridded-Response: Fill in the grid with your answer to each question.

11. A circular garden is to be edged with stone pavers. The garden has a diameter of 9 feet. Stone pavers are 8 inches long. About how many stone pavers will be needed to edge the garden?

Extended-Response: Show your work.

12. The diameter of a circle is 12 in. What is the area of $\frac{1}{4}$ of the circle?

MN Test Prep Grade 9

GEOMETRY

Congruent Triangles

9.11.13 Solve problems using triangle congruence. Also 9.11.16, V.B.1

Select the best answer for each question.

1. Which choice completes the congruence statement?

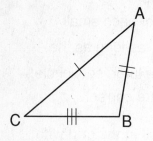

$$\overline{AC} \cong \underline{\hspace{2cm}}$$

A. $\overline{DE}$ **C.** $\overline{DF}$

B. $\overline{FE}$ **D.** $\overline{DF}$

2. Which theorem proves that the two triangles are congruent?

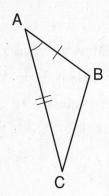
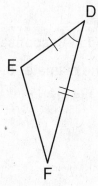

A. SSS   **C.** AAS

B. SAS   **D.** HL

3. Which of the three triangles below can be proven congruent by SSS or SAS?

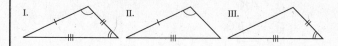

A. I and II

B. II and III

C. I and III

D. I

4. What is the perimeter of polygon *ABCD*?

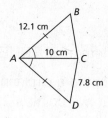

A. 29.9 cm

B. 39.8 cm

C. 49.8 cm

D. 59.9 cm

5. Jacob wants to prove that $\triangle FGH \cong \triangle JKL$ using SAS. He knows that $\overline{FG} \cong \overline{JK}$ and $\overline{FH} \cong \overline{JL}$. What additional piece of information does he need?

A. $\angle F \cong \angle J$

B. $\angle G \cong \angle K$

C. $\angle H \cong \angle L$

D. $\angle F \cong \angle G$

Name_____ Date _____ Class_____

Use the diagram to answer questions 6 and 7.

6. A quilt pattern of a dog is shown here. $ML = MP = MN = MQ = 1$ inch

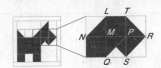

Which statement is correct?

A. $\triangle LMN \cong \triangle QMP$ by SAS

B. $\triangle LMN \cong \triangle QMP$ by SSS

C. $\triangle LMN \cong \triangle MQP$ by SAS

D. $\triangle LMN \cong \triangle MQP$ by SSS

7. P is the midpoint of $\overline{TS}$ and $TR = SR = 1.4$ inches. What can you conclude about $\triangle TRP$ and $\triangle SRP$?

A. $\triangle TRP = \triangle SRP$

B. $\triangle TRP \cong \triangle SRP$

C. They are similar triangles.

D. $\overline{TR} \cong \overline{TS}$

8. What additional congruence statement is necessary to prove $\triangle XWY \cong \triangle XVZ$ by ASA?

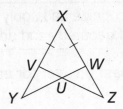

A. $\angle XVZ \cong \angle XWY$

B. $\angle VUY \cong \angle WUZ$

C. $\overline{VZ} \cong \overline{WY}$

D. $\overline{XZ} \cong \overline{XY}$

Gridded-Response: Fill in the grid with your answer to each question.

9. What must the value of x be to prove that $\triangle EFG \triangle EHG$ by SSS?

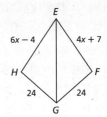

Extended-Response: Show your work.

10. Which postulate or theorem justifies the congruence statement $\triangle STU \cong \triangle VUT$? Explain your answer.

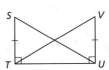

MN Test Prep Grade 9

GEOMETRY

Logical Reasoning

9.11.17 Recognize and apply mathematical and geometric axioms, fundamental theorems of geometry and ddeductive reasoning. Also 9.11.16, 9.11.18 I.A.4

Select the best answer for each question.

1. $\overline{HF}$ bisects $\angle EHG$. Which conclusion is NOT valid?

   A. E, F, and G are coplanar.
   B. $\angle EHF \cong \angle FHG$
   C. $\overline{EF} \cong \overline{FG}$
   D. $m\angle EHF \cong m\angle FHG$

2. Which of the following conclusions can be drawn from the given information?

   Given: If one angle of a triangle is 90°, then the triangle is a right triangle. If a triangle is a right triangle, then its acute angle measures are complementary.

   A.   If one angle of a triangle is 90°, then its acute angle measures are complementary.
   B. If one angle of a triangle is 90°, then its acute angle measures are supplementary.
   C. If one angle of a triangle is 90°, then it is a right triangle.
   D. If the acute angle measures of a triangle are complementary, then one angle of a triangle is 90°.

3. Which conclusion is not valid given two angles ($\angle A$ and $\angle C$) in a triangle ABC are congruent so the triangle is isosceles?

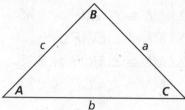

   A. the sides opposite the congruent angles are congruent.
   B. the base angles are congruent
   C. side a = side b
   D. side a = side c

4. Given the points $D(1, 5)$ and $E(-2, 3)$ which conclusion is not valid?

   A. The midpoint of $\overline{DE}$ is $(-2, 4)$.
   B. $\overline{DE} \cong \overline{ED}$
   C. D and E are distinct points.
   D. The distance between D and E is $\sqrt{5}$.

5. What conclusion CANNOT be drawn about this pair of congruent figures?

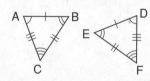

   A. These triangles are identical in shape.
   B. $\angle ACB = \angle EDF$
   C. $\angle ABC = \angle DEF$
   D. $\triangle ABC$ could be translated to coincide exactly with $\triangle DEF$.

64

6. Two adjoining fields are triangular in shape. The one field has sides measuring 30 meters, 50 meters and 40 meters. The second field has corresponding sides measuring 30 meters, 50 meters and 40 meters. What CANNOT be said about these two fields?

A. They are congruent.

B. The corresponding angles will be congruent.

C. They cover the identical amount of ground.

D. One field would exactly fit over the other field.

Use the diagram of the kite for questions 7 and 8.

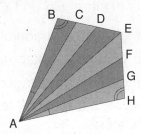

$\overline{AE}$ is the angle bisector of $\angle DAF$ and $\angle DEF$.

7. Which of the following can be concluded about $\triangle DEA$ and $\triangle FEA$?

I $\triangle DEA \cong \triangle FEA$

II $\overline{DE} = \overline{EF}$

III $\overline{CE} = \overline{EG}$

A. I only   C. III only

B. II only   D. I and II

Gridded-Response: Fill in the grid with your answer to each question.

8. If $\overline{AB}$ and $\overline{AH}$ are equal, and the perimeter of $\triangle ABC$ is 10 cm, what is the perimeter of $\triangle AHG$??

Extended-Response: Show your work.

9. In the figure below, $m\angle 1 = m\angle 2$. What is the value of y?

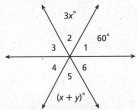

Note: Figure not drawn to scale

MN Test Prep Grade 9

GEOMETRY

Plane Figures

9.11.05 Identify, apply, or solve problems that require knowledge of geometric properties of plane figures (e.g., tringles, quadrilaterals, parallel lines cut by a transversal, angles, diagonals, triangle inequality). V.B.3

Select the best answer for each question.

Use this parallelogram for questions 1–3.

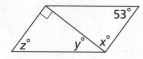

1. What is the measure of *x*?

   A. 25°

   B. 45°

   C. 75°

   D. 90°

2. What is the measure of *y*?

   A. 37°

   B. 45°

   C. 90°

   D. 110°

3. What is the measure of *z*?

   A. 37°

   B. 45°

   C. 53°

   D. 90°

Use this figure for questions 4 and 5.

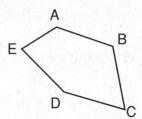

4. What do you get if you connect the midpoints of sides $\overline{BC}$ and $\overline{CD}$?

   A. A triangle and a quadrilateral

   B. A triangle and a hexagon

   C. A triangle and an octagon

   D. A triangle, a trapezoid, and a quadrilateral

5. Which term describes the figures you get when you connect vertex *C* with the midpoint of side $\overline{EA}$?

   A. Congruent

   B. Symmetric

   C. Proportional

   D. Quadrilaterals

    MN Test Prep Grade 9

6. $\overline{PR}$ divides the square into

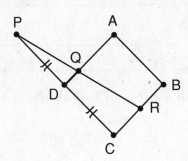

A. Trapezoids   **C.** Pentagons

B. Triangles   **D.** Rectangles

7. Which polygon has 11 sides?

A.

B.

C.

D.

8. Which is a concave figure?

A.

B.

C.

D.

9. Which figure is impossible?

   A. A parallelogram with opposite sides equal

   B. A rhombus with opposite angles equal

   C. A triangle with 2 right angles

   D. All of the above are possible

Gridded-Response: Fill in the grid with your answer to each question.

10. What is the sum of angles in a quadrilateral?

Extended-Response: Show your work.

11. Which of the following CANNOT be a result of drawing a diagonal in a pentagon: square, triangle, hexagon, quadrilateral pentagon? Justify your answer with illustrations.

GEOMETRY

Special Right Triangles

9.11.20 Solve problems using 45°, -45°, -90° and 30°, -60°, -90° triangles. V.B.3

Select the best answer for each question.

Use this figure for questions 1 and 2.

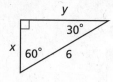

1. Find the value of *x*.

   A. 2

   B. 3

   C. 6

   D. 9

2. Find the value of *y*.

   A. $3\sqrt{3}$

   B. 3

   C. 6

   D. 9

3. An 18-inch diagonal of a rectangular picture frame creates a 30°-60°-90° triangle. What is the length of the longest side of the picture frame?

   A. 9.00 in.

   B. 15.59 in.

   C. 20.78 in.

   D. 31.18 in.

Use this figure for questions 4 and 5.

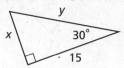

4. Find the value of *x*.

   A. $\sqrt{3}$

   B. 5

   C. $5\sqrt{3}$

   D. $10\sqrt{3}$

5. Find the value of *y*.

   A. $\sqrt{3}$

   B. 5

   C. $5\sqrt{3}$

   D. $10\sqrt{3}$

6. A 45°-45°-90° triangle has a hypotenuse that is 15 inches. Find the length of each side.

   A. 5.8 inches

   B. 9.6 inches

   C. 10.6 inches

   D. 12.8 inches

 MN Test Prep Grade 9

7. Which is statement is true?

    A. In a 45°-45°-90° triangle, both legs are congruent.

    B. In a 45°-45°-90° triangle, the length of the hypotenuse is 2 times the length of a leg.

    C. A 45°-45°-90° triangle is equilateral.

    D. In a 45°-45°-90° triangle, the length of the longer leg is 2 times the length of the shorter leg.

8. Which statement is false?

    A. A 30°-60°-90° triangle is a scalene triangle.

    B. In a 30°-60°-90° triangle, the length of the hypotenuse is 2 times the length of the shorter leg.

    C. In a 30°-60°-90° triangle, the length of the hypotenuse is $\sqrt{3}$ times the longer leg.

    D. In a 30°-60°-90° triangle, the length of the longer leg is the length of the short leg times $\sqrt{3}$.

Gridded-Response: Fill in the grid with your answer to each question.

9. A 45°-45°-90° triangle has a leg that is 10 cm. Find the approximate length of the hypotenuse in centimeters.

10. Regulation billiard balls are $2\frac{1}{4}$ in. in diameter. The rack used to group 15 billiard balls is in the shape of an equilateral triangle. What is the approximate height of the triangle formed by the rack? Round your answer to the nearest quarter inch.

Extended-Response: Show your work for each question.

Use this figure for questions 11 and 12.

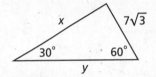

11. Find the value of x.

12. Find the value of y.

GEOMETRY

Trigonometry

9.11.22 Define, identify, and evaluate trigometric ratios. V.B.4

Select the best answer for each question.

Figures are not drawn to scale.

Use the right triangle below for questions 1–3.

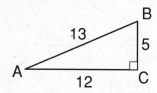

1. What is the sine of ∠A?

   A. $\frac{12}{13}$

   B. $\frac{5}{12}$

   C. $\frac{5}{13}$

   D. $\frac{13}{12}$

2. What is the cosine of ∠A?

   A. $\frac{12}{13}$

   B. $\frac{5}{12}$

   C. $\frac{5}{13}$

   D. $\frac{13}{12}$

3 What is the tangent of ∠A?

   A. $\frac{12}{13}$ C. $\frac{5}{13}$

   B. $\frac{5}{12}$ D. $\frac{13}{12}$

4. What is the length of the unknown side of the right triangle? Round your answer to the nearest hundredth.

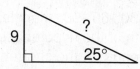

   A. 8.16

   B. 9.93

   C. 19.3

   D. 21.30

5. The length of side *a* is 24. The tangent of ∠A is $\frac{12}{5}$. What is the length of the hypotenuse?

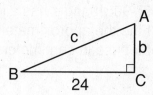

   A. 5   C. 26

   B. 12   D. $\sqrt{313}$

6. Which of the following has the same value as sin *A*?

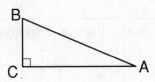

A. sin *B*   **C.** cos *B*

B. cos *A*   **D.** tan *A*

7. What is the length of the unknown side of the right triangle below? Round your answer to the nearest hundredth.

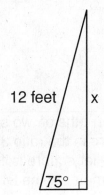

A. 3.11 feet   **C.** 10.42 feet

B. 9.32 feet   **D.** 11.59 feet

8. Which trigonometric identities are true?

I $\sec^2 \theta = 1 + \tan^2 \theta$

II $\sec \theta = \dfrac{1}{\sin \theta}$

III $\sin^2 \theta + \cos^2 \theta = 1$

IV $\tan \theta = \dfrac{\cos \theta}{\sin \theta}$

A. I and II are true.

B. I and III are true.

C. I and IV are true

D. II and IV are true.

Gridded-Response: Fill in the grid with your answer to each question.

9. Find the measure of *PR* to the nearest tenth.

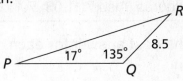

10. Find the measure of ∠*X* to the nearest degree.

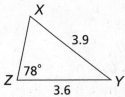

Extended-Response: Show your work.

11. A boat is pulling a parasailer. The line to the parasailer is 1200 feet long. The angle between the line and the water is about 32°. How high is the parasailer? Round to the nearest foot.

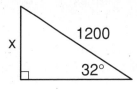

MN Test Prep Grade 9

MEASUREMENT

Perimeter, Circumference, and Area

7.11.05 Determine the linear measure, perimeter, area, surface area, and volume of similar figures. Also 7.11.03, 7.11.04, 7.11.06, V.B.3

Select the best answer for each question.

1. Which rectangle is similar to one with dimensions of 3.2 meters and 7.2 meters?

    A. 2 m by 4 m

    B. 2 m by 4.5 m

    C. 2.5 m by 4 m

    D. 2.5 m by 4.5 m

2. Two right triangles are similar and their ratio of corresponding sides is 1 : x. What is the ratio of their areas?

    A. 1 : x

    B. 1 : $2x$

    C. 1 : x^2

    D. 1 : $2x^2$

3. Two acute triangles are similar and their ratio of corresponding sides is 1 : y. What is the ratio of perimeters?

    A. 1 : y

    B. 1 : $2y$

    C. 1 : $3y$

    D. 1 : y^2

4. Figures A and B are similar figures. One side of A has a length of 9 cm, and the corresponding side of B has a length of 12 cm. The three other sides of A have lengths of 6 cm, 12 cm, and 3 cm. What is NOT a possible length of the sides of B?

    A. 8 cm

    B. 16 cm

    C. 9 cm

    D. 4 cm

5. The side lengths of two similar squares are in the ratio 3 : 2. One side of the smaller square is 12 cm. What is the perimeter of the larger square?

    A. 8 cm

    B.. 48 cm

    C. 36 cm

    D. 72 cm

6. Rectangle A has dimensions 3.6 meters by 7.2 meters. Rectangle B is similar to rectangle A and has a width of 1.8 meters. Which is the length of rectangle B?

    A. 7.2 m

    B. 0.9 m

    C. 3.6 m

    D. 4.8 m

7. The lengths of corresponding sides of similar rectangles are in the ratio 5 : 2. The perimeter of the smaller rectangle is 40 feet. What is the perimeter of the larger rectangle?

   A. 16 feet

   B. 100 feet

   C. 500 feet

   D. 50 feet

8. Find the value of x that makes the two right triangles similar.

 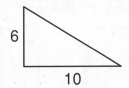

   A. 4.2

   B. 4.3

   C. 4.4

   D. 4.5

9. The ratio of the corresponding sides of 2 similar triangles is 2 : 6. The sides of the larger triangle are 12 yards, 15 yards, and 18 yards. What is the perimeter of the smaller triangle?

   A. 7.5 yards

   B. 12 yards

   C. 15 yards

   D. 25 yards

10. Mr. and Mrs. Kingston are installing fence around their property. The length of the property is 780 yards and the width is 520 yards. How many yards of fencing are needed?

   A. 1,300 yards

   B. 1,560 yards

   C. 2,600 yards

   D. 2,860 yards

11. The figures are similar. What is the value of n?

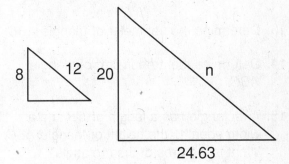

   A. 4.8

   B. 30

   C. 32

   D. 48

12. Determine the area of the circle. (Use $\pi = 3.14$.)

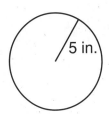

   A. 39.25 in^2 **C.** 157 in^2

   B. 78.5 in^2 **D.** 314 in^2

Name_____ Date _____ Class_____

Gridded-Response: Fill in the grid with your answer to each question.

Use the figure shown below for questions 13–15.

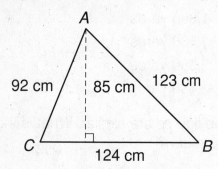

92 cm   85 cm   123 cm

124 cm

C   B   A

13. Determine the perimeter of triangle *ABC*.

14. Determine the area in cm² of triangle *ABC*.

15. A rectangle has a length of *CB* and a width equal to the height of triangle *ABC*. What is the area of the rectangle?

16. Find the perimeter (in inches). of the figure.

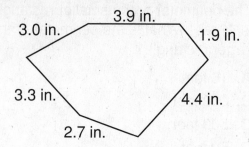

3.9 in.
3.0 in.   1.9 in.
3.3 in.   4.4 in.
2.7 in.

Extended-Response: Show your work.

17.

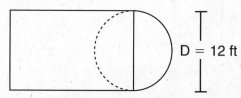

19 ft

D = 12 ft

A. Consider the portion of a basketball court shown above, known as the "key." What is the area and perimeter of this region? Explain your answer.

B. A standard basketball court has two keys, one at each end. The dimensions of the entire court are 94 feet by 50 feet. What is the area of the court, NOT including both keys?

MEASUREMENT

Perimeter, Surface Area, and Volume

> 7.11.05 Determine the linear measure, perimeter, area, and volume of similar figures.
> Also 7.11.03, 7.11.04, 7.11.06, V.B.3

Select the best answer for each question.

1. What is the surface area of this figure made by gluing five identical cubes together?

   3 cm

   A. 66 square centimeters
   B. 198 square centimeters
   C. 216 square centimeters
   D. 270 square centimeters

2. A rectangular prism is 2 inches × 4 inches × 6 inches. Another rectangular prism has dimensions that are three times as long. How much greater is the volume of the second prism than the first prism?

   A. 6 times
   B. 9 times
   C. 18 times
   D. 27 times

3. What is the surface area of the given figure?

   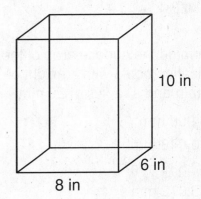

   10 in

   6 in

   8 in

   A. 168 square inches
   B. 216 square inches
   C. 240 square inches
   D. 376 square inches

4. Determine the volume of a waffle cone with height 18 cm and radius of 5 cm. Round to the nearest cubic centimeter.

   A. 188 cm^3 **C.** 471 cm^3
   B. 282 cm^3 **D.** 1413 cm^3

5. Determine the volume of a sphere with a radius of 2 ft. $\left(\text{Hint: } V = \dfrac{4\pi r^3}{3}\right)$.

   A. 16.75 ft^3
   B. 33.49 ft^3
   C. 50.24 ft^3
   D. 110.48 ft^3

Name_____ Date _____ Class_____

Use the figure shown for questions 6 and 7.

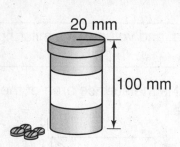

20 mm

100 mm

6. Determine the surface area of the medication bottle with a height of 100 mm and a radius of 20 mm.

   A. 6,908 mm^2

   B. 10,048 mm^2

   C. 12,560 mm^2

   D. 15,072 mm^2

7. Determine the volume of the medicine bottle.

   A. 1,256 mm^3

   B. 31,400 mm^3

   C. 125,600 mm^3

   D. 131,880 mm^3

8. Determine the surface area of one fair die if one side length is 2 inches.

   A. 24 in^2

   B. 16 in^2

   C. 8 in^2

   D. 6 in^2

9. According to question 8, what is the volume of both fair dice?

   A. 4 in^3

   B. 6 in^3

   C. 8 in^3

   D. 16 in^3

Use the figure shown below for questions 10 and 11.

$2\frac{1}{4}$ ft

$\frac{1}{3}$ ft $\frac{1}{2}$ ft

10. What is the surface area of the gift?

   A. 3 ft^2

   B. $4\frac{1}{12}$ ft^2

   C. $2\frac{1}{12}$ ft^2

   D. $2\frac{1}{6}$ ft^2

11. What is the volume of the gift?

   A. $\frac{3}{8}$ ft^3

   B. $\frac{5}{8}$ ft^3

   C. $1\frac{1}{8}$ ft^3

   D. $3\frac{3}{8}$ ft^3

Name_____ Date _____ Class_____

12. A cylindrical shaped container is 18 centimeters tall and has circular bases with radii of 3 centimeters. What is the volume of the cylinder?

A. 108π cm^3

B. 81π cm^3

C. 162π cm^3

D. 324π cm^3

Use the figure shown for questions 13 and 14.

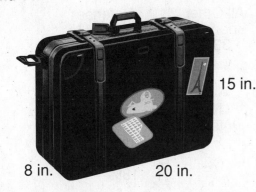

15 in.

8 in.   20 in.

13. Find the volume of Valerie's suitcase. (Hint: $V = \ell wh$)

14. Find the surface area of Valerie's suitcase (in inches).

15. The following diagram is a map of the walking trail at Oak Openings Park. Find the length of the walking trail.

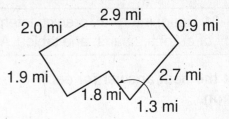

2.9 mi

2.0 mi   0.9 mi

1.9 mi   2.7 mi

1.8 mi

1.3 mi

Extended-Response: Show your work.

16. A cylindrical storage tank rests in a hole shaped like a rectangular prism, as shown below:

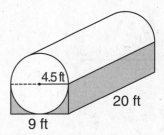

4.5 ft

20 ft

9 ft

A. Explain how you would find the volume of the space not occupied by the tank, shown shaded in the figure.

B. Compare the volume of liquid in the tank when it is half-full to the volume you found in part A.

DATA ANALYSIS AND PROBABILITY

Displays of Data

10.11.01 Read, interpret, predict, interpolate, extrapolate, and use information froma variety of graphs, charts, and tables. Also 10.11.02, 10.11.03 IV.A.1

Select the best answer for each question.

1. Which scatter plot shows a positive correlation between two variables for a set of data?

A.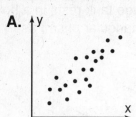

B.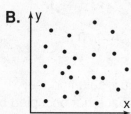

C.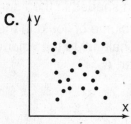

D.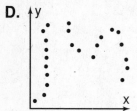

Use the circle graph to answer questions 2 and 3.

Government Spending for Fiscal Year 2002

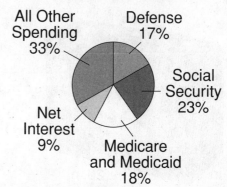

2. Which is not a true statement about this graph?

A. This is a circle graph that shows the spending of the government for fiscal year 2002.

B. The government spent 23% of its revenue on Medicare and Medicaid.

C. The largest region on the circle graph corresponds to the category "All Other Spending."

D. The smallest region represents "Net Interest."

3. For each dollar the federal government spent in 2002, how much was spent on Social Security and Medicare/Medicaid?

A. $0.18   C. $0.35

B. $0.25   D. $0.41

Name_____ Date _____ Class _____

Use the bar graph to answer questions 4 and 5.

The graph shows the number of televisions in randomly selected households.

Number of Televisions in Households

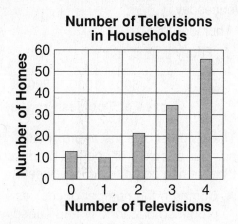

4. What is the approximate difference between the number of households who owned 3 televisions and those who owned one?

A. 12   C. 30

B. 24   D. 35

5. Which statement is not supported by this chart?

A. The number of households that have two televisions is more than 20.

B. The number of households that have 1 television is greater than the number of households which have no televisions.

C. The number of households that have 4 televisions is greater than the number of households which have 3 televisions.

D. No household has 7 televisions.

Use the graph to answer questions 6 and 7.

Price per share of Busy Motors, Inc. Stock

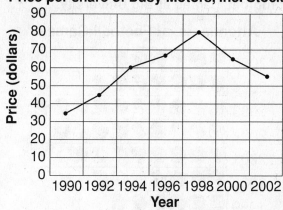

6. What is the approximate value of the stock for the year 1995?

A. $63   C. $72

B. $68   D. $75

7. During which period was the stock price decreasing?

A. 1990–2002   C. 1990–1998

B. 1996–2001   D. 1998–2002

8. According to this Venn diagram, to which set do rhombuses NOT belong?

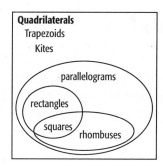

A. Parallelograms

B. Rectangles

C. Squares

D. Both B and C

MN Test Prep Grade 9

Use the pictogram to answer questions 9 and 10.

The graph shows the average attendance at football games at Big University.

Attendance at Football Games

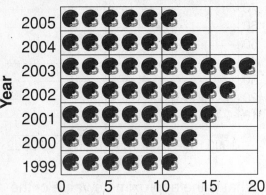

Number of People (thousands)

🏈 = 2,000 people

9. The university received extra funding for its football program if the average attendance was over 16,000. For which years did the university receive extra funding?

   A. 1999, 2000

   B. 2001

   C. 2002, 2003

   D. 2004, 2005

Gridded-Response: Fill in the grid with your answer to each question.

10. What is the difference in thousands between the most people attending and the fewest people attending?

Extended-Response: Show your work.

Use the bar chart to answer question 11.

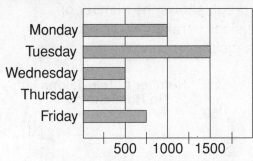

Boxes of Cookies Produced

11. The graph shows the approximate number of boxes of cookies produced by a baking company in one week.

   A. Compare the number of cookies produced on Monday and Tuesday with the number produced during the rest of the week.

   B. Based on the data chart, draw a valid conclusion about the number of boxes of cookies produced throughout the week. Justify your conclusion.

MN Test Prep Grade 9

DATA ANALYSIS AND PROBABILITY

Measures of Data

> 10.11.05 Calculate, interpret, and use measures of central tendency and dispersion.
> Also 10.11.04 and 10.11.06, IV.A.2

Select the best answer for each question.

Use the data given below to answer questions 1–4.

96, 99, 106, 106, 124, 132, 137, 144

1. Find the range of the data.

   A. 45
   B. 46
   C. 47
   D. 48

2. Find the median of the data.

   A. 106
   B. 115
   C. 118
   D. 124

3. Find the mode of the data.

   A. 106
   B. 115
   C. 118
   D. 124

4. Find the mean of the data.

   A. 106   C. 118
   B. 115   D. 124

Use the information to answer questions 5–7.

Christopher's test scores for his economics class have a mean of 86 with a range of 25.

5. The sum of Christopher's test scores is 516. How many tests has he taken?

   A. 3
   B. 4
   C. 5
   D. 6

6. Christopher's lowest test score is 68. What is his highest test score?

   A. 43
   B. 78
   C. 83
   D. 93

7. If Christopher gets an average of 90, he will win a scholarship. If he gets 100 on all of his next tests, how many more tests will it take to get his average above 90?

   A. 1
   B. 2
   C. 3
   D. 4

Use the data set {10, 10, 10, 20, 30, 35} to answer questions 8 and 9.

8. Which statement is true about this data set?

   A. The median is 20.
   B. The mode is 30.
   C. There is no mode.
   D. The range is 25.

9. Which statement is not true about this data set?

   A. The mean is 20.
   B. The range is equal to the median plus 10.
   C. The mode is equal to the minimum value.
   D. The mode is equal to 10.

10. Which number, if added to the data set, would affect the mean the most for this data set?

    {11, 98, 23, 18, 29, 9, 15}

    A. 29
    B. 98
    C. 11
    D. 15

11. Which value best describes this set of data?

    {11, 98, 23, 18, 29, 9, 15}

    A. Mean
    B. Median
    C. Minimum value
    D. Mode

12. Identify the measure of central tendency that is being used in this statement.

    The average test score in mathematics for Chase Elementary school is 84.

    A. Mean
    B. Median
    C. Mode
    D. Range

13. Identify the measure of central tendency that is being used in this statement.

    Mitchell's salary is larger than that of half of the employees at the company where he works.

    A. Mean
    B. Median
    C. Mode
    D. Percentile

14. What is the inter-quartile range of the following data?

    2, 3, 5, 7, 11, 13, 17, 19, 23, 29, 31

    A. 5
    B. 13
    C. 18
    D. 29

Name_____ Date _____ Class_____

Use the data to answer questions 15–18. The following data are the weights (in pounds) of eight competition dogs.

123, 145, 105, 98, 130, 111, 87, 105

15. Find the range of the data.
   A. 45
   B. 58
   C. 63
   D. 70

16 Find the median of the data.
   A. 105
   B. 108
   C. 110.5
   D. 126.5

17. Find the mode of the data.
   A. 98
   B. 100
   C. 105
   D. 123

18. Find the mean of the data.
   A. 98
   B. 100
   C. 110
   D. 113

Gridded-Response: Fill in the grid with your answer to each question.

Use the information to answer questions 19 and 20.

Sara's test scores for her anatomy class have a mean of 96 with a range of 8.

19. The sum of Sara's test scores is 576. How many tests has she taken?

20. Sara's highest test score is 98. What is her lowest test score?

Extended-Response: Show your work.

21. The weekly salaries of the employees in an office are $1,000, $1,150, $1,200, $1,250, and $4,000.
   A. The manager tells a candidate for a job that the average salary is $1,720. Why is this misleading?
   B. What would be a more appropriate measure of central tendency to use? Explain your answer.

DATA ANALYSIS AND PROBABILITY

Surveys and Samples

> 9.D3.4 Understand how samples statistics reflect the values of population parameters and use sampling distributions as the basis for informal inference. Also 9.D1.4, 9.D1.5, 9.D1.6, IV.B.5

Select the best answer for each question.

1. Marcus makes a list of numbers by repeatedly spinning the spinner shown below.

   If there are 200 numbers in the list, about how many of the numbers would you expect to be 3?

   A. 25   C. 100

   B. 50   D. 150

2. Betsy is in charge of a food booth at a school carnival. She wants to conduct a survey of people to find out their favorite ice cream flavors. Which question would most likely lead to unbiased results?

   A. Do you like vanilla, chocolate, or strawberry ice cream?

   B. What are your top three favorite ice cream flavors (e.g., vanilla, chocolate, strawberry)?

   C. What are your three favorite ice cream flavors?

   D. Can you name three ice cream flavors?

3. Two-thirds of the paints in an art studio are watercolors and the rest are acrylic. If 120 paints are selected randomly from the cabinet, how many would you expect to be acrylic?

   A. 40   C. 60

   B. 80   D. 90

4. Michelle spins the spinner shown below 14 times.

   Which of the following results is least likely to have been produced by this spinner?

   A. 3 1s, 3 2s, 4 3s, and 4 4s

   B. 3 1s, 3 2s, 3 3s, and 5 4s

   C. 2 1s, 5 2s, 4 3s, and 3 4s

   D. 3 1s, 0 2s, 8 3s, and 3 4s

5. Gerald wants to create a sequence of ones, twos, and threes randomly in such a way that the three digits each have an equal probability of appearing. Which of the following methods will produce this result?

   A. Flip two coins; if there are two heads, write "3"; if there is one head, write "2"; if there are no heads, write "1."

   B. Write the number "1" on three slips of paper, the number "2" on two slips of paper, and the number "3" on four slips of paper, and place them in a bag. Randomly pull a slip from the bag, record the number, and replace the slip.

   C. Roll a number cube; if a 1, 2, or 3 is rolled, use that number, otherwise roll again.

   D. Count to three and when three is reached, immediately hold out one, two, or three fingers of the right hand and write down how many fingers were held out.

6. Vassia wants to conduct a survey to find out the average number of hours a day people spend reading. Which method is most likely to give her accurate results?

A. Hand out a questionnaire to people at the public library.

B. Hand out a questionnaire to people at a bookstore.

C. Ask everybody in the town whose first name begins with the letter "M."

D. Study the records at the public library to find out how long most books remain checked out.

7. On an island, people introduced mongooses to control the snake population. Officials surveyed the land to count the size of the population of mongooses and snakes, starting in the year that the mongooses were introduced. The data are shown in the chart.

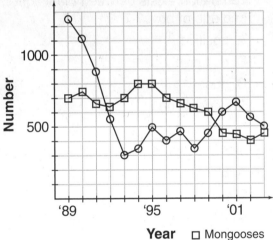

Year □ Mongooses
○ Snakes

Which of the following statements is true?

A. The snake population declined rapidly, then leveled out at roughly a third its original size.

B. The snake population declined slightly, but not a lot.

C. The snake population was temporarily disrupted but recovered completely.

D. The snake population was not affected and remained at about the same level throughout.

8. April would like to know what people's favorite hamburger toppings are. She sits at a local hamburger joint and records the toppings that people order. What is one of the problems with this experiment?

A. The hamburger joint might not have a representative sample of toppings.

B. April should have gone to a general cafeteria instead of a hamburger joint.

C. Not everyone who goes to a hamburger joint orders a hamburger.

D. April should include people who do not eat hamburgers.

Gridded-Response: Fill in the grid with your answer to each question.

9. Parker wants to estimate the number of tiles on his kitchen floor. He measures that the floor is a rectangle 10 feet by 12 feet. In one square foot, he counts about 60 tiles. About how many tiles cover the kitchen floor?

Extended-Response: Show your work.

10. To find out how many students at an elementary school have had chicken pox, the principal surveyed all of the first graders.

A. What is wrong with this sample?

B. What would be a better sampling method?

DATA ANALYSIS AND PROBABILITY

Scatterplots and Lines of Best Fit

9.D2.4 Interpret and analyze data from graphical representations and draw simple conclusions (e.g., line of best fit). Also 9.D1.1, 9.D1.2, 9.D1.3, 9.D2.1, 9.D2.2, 9.D2.3, 9.D2.5, 9.D2.7, 9.D2.8, 9.D3.1, 9.D3.2, 9.D3.3 IV.A.3

Select the best answer for each question.

1. Harold did an experiment to see if reflex times are affected by age. He collected data and made the scatterplot of his data shown below.

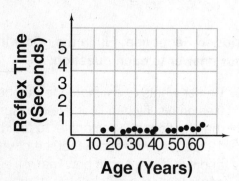

He concludes that reflex times remain fast and unaffected by age. Which of the following choices describes a problem with the scatterplot that Harold made?

A. He did not include all the data he collected.

B. The axes are not properly labeled.

C. The vertical scale is not appropriately chosen.

D. The horizontal scale is not appropriately chosen.

2. Which does NOT increase the accuracy of a scatterplot

A. more data

B. expanded vertical scale

C. expanded horizontal scale

D. another variable

For problems 3–5 refer to the scatterplot below which shows the heights and ages of a number of boys.

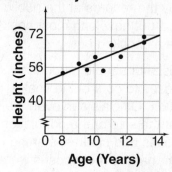

3. Based on the graph, what kind of correlation exists between the height and age of boys?

A. positive

B. negative

C. none

D. perfect linear

4. Based on the graph, how tall would you expect an average 11-year-old boy to be?

A. 56 in.

B. 62 in.

C. 69 in.

D. 72 in.

5. If the trend in the chart were to continue, how tall would you expect a 20-year-old to be?

A. 74 in.

B. 80 in.

C. 86 in.

D. 92 in.

Name_____ Date _____ Class_____

Use the scatterplot to answer questions 6 and 7.

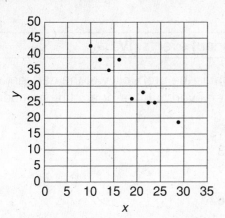

6. Which of the following graphs best describes the relationship between the variables x and y?

A.
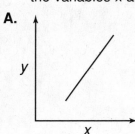

C.
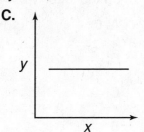

B.
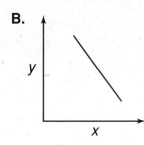

D.
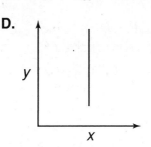

Gridded-Response: Fill in the grid with your answer to each question.

7. What is the value of y when $x = 10$?

Extended-Response: Show your work for each question.

8. Use the scatterplot with its trend line to answer parts A and B.

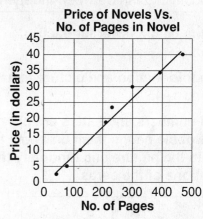

Price of Novels Vs. No. of Pages in Novel

A. Describe the relationship between the number of pages in a novel and its price.

B. What is the difference between the price for a 300-page novel on the trend line and the actual price of a 300-page novel? Describe, in words, how you found this answer.

DATA ANALYSIS AND PROBABILITY

Theoretical Probabilty

9.D4.4 Distinguish between independent and dependent events. IV.B.4

Select the best answer for each question.

Use the information and picture to answer questions 1–4.

Several numbers and letters are put on cards. Bobbie hangs them on a wall as shown in the picture and randomly throws a dart at one of the cards.

5	A	3	S
B	Z	8	M
N	7	2	U
E	Q	P	12

1. What is the probability of the dart landing on a vowel or on an even number?

   A. $\frac{1}{5}$

   B. $\frac{5}{16}$

   C. $\frac{3}{8}$

   D. $\frac{7}{16}$

2. What is the probability of the dart landing on a consonant?

   A. $\frac{4}{25}$

   B. $\frac{3}{8}$

   C. $\frac{7}{16}$

   D. $\frac{7}{8}$

3. What is the probability of the dart landing on an even number or a prime number?

   A. $\frac{3}{16}$

   B. $\frac{3}{8}$

   C. $\frac{5}{64}$

   D. $\frac{11}{18}$

4. What is the probability of the dart landing on the letter V?

   A. 0

   B. $\frac{3}{64}$

   C. $\frac{1}{4}$

   D. $\frac{9}{16}$

5. Which pair of events is NOT mutually exclusive?

   A. Getting a 4 and getting an odd number when rolling one number cube

   B. Drawing a king and drawing a heart when drawing one card from a deck of playing cards

   C. Drawing a red card and drawing a black card when drawing one card from a deck of playing cards

   D. Getting a 5 and getting a 1 when rolling a number cube

6. Which experiment has the sample space: {1-heads, 2-heads, 3-heads, 4-heads, 5-heads, 6-heads, 1-tails, 2-tails, 3-tails, 4-tails, 5-tails, 6-tails}?

A. Roll a die two times

B. Toss a coin three times

C. Toss a coin two times

D. Roll a die and then toss a coin

Use the following information to answer questions 7–10.

A school has 60 teachers. Of the 40 male teachers, 2 teach history. One-twelfth of all the teachers at the school teach history.

7. What is the probability that a teacher is a female or teaches history?

A. $\frac{11}{30}$

B. $\frac{7}{12}$

C. $\frac{41}{60}$

D. $\frac{43}{60}$

8. What is the probability that a teacher is a man?

A. $\frac{2}{3}$

B. $\frac{57}{60}$

C. $\frac{13}{60}$

D. $\frac{1}{3}$

9. What is the probability that a teacher is a man or does not teach history?

A. $\frac{7}{12}$

B. $\frac{57}{60}$

C. $\frac{1}{20}$

D. $\frac{1}{12}$

10. What is the probability that a teacher does not teach history?

A. $\frac{1}{20}$

B. $\frac{1}{12}$

C. $\frac{11}{12}$

D. $\frac{7}{12}$

11. If you were to randomly choose a letter between *G* and *P* (inclusive), what is the probability that the letter will be a vowel?

A. $\frac{1}{5}$

B. $\frac{1}{10}$

C. $\frac{1}{4}$

D. $\frac{1}{8}$

Name_____ Date _____ Class_____

Gridded-Response: Fill in the grid with your answer to each question.

Use the information to answer questions 12–15.

Each resident of a town casts one vote for chairperson of the library board. Of the residents, 35% voted for Smith, 20% voted for Masters, 25% voted for Hill, and 20% voted for Green. A surveyor selected residents at random and asked how they voted.

12. What is the probability that a randomly chosen resident voted for Smith or Hill?

13. What is the probability that a randomly chosen resident did not vote for Green?

14. What is the probability that a randomly chosen resident voted for neither Masters nor Hill?

15. What is the probability that someone voted against Smith?

Extended-Response: Show your work.

16. A company has 2 reserved parking spaces to raffle off every month. Each month, 12 employees enter the raffle.

   A. What is the average number of times per year that each employee in the raffle wins a parking space?

   B. If 2 more employees enter the raffle, how is the probability of winning affected?

MN Test Prep Grade 9

Name_____ Date _____ Class_____

SAMPLE TEST A

Select the best answer for each question.

1. What is the value of the expression $|-3| - 8 + |-5|$?

  A. -6

  B. $|-6|$

  C. 0

  D. $|6|$

2. Chris earns \$7.85 per hour teaching math. He needs at least \$40 to buy some CDs. Which inequality would you use to find out how many hours, *h*, Chris needs to teach?

  A. $7.85h > 40$

  B. $7.85h \le 40$

  C. $7.85h \ge 40$

  D. $7.85h < 40$

3. Darren plans to plant 52 bulbs. He has one bag of twelve daffodil bulbs. He plans to buy hyacinth bulbs in bags that contain four bulbs each. How many bags of hyacinth bulbs should he buy?

  A. 8

  B. 9

  C. 10

  D. 12

4. Which figure shows a circle inscribed in a right triangle?

  A.

  B.

  C.

  D. Both B and C show a circle inscribed in a right triangle.

5. A twelve-foot-long ladder leans against the side of a building. The base of the ladder makes an angle of 75° with the horizontal. How high up the building does the ladder reach? Round your answer to the nearest hundredth.

  A. 9.32 feet

  B. 10.42 feet

  C. 11.02 feet

  D. 11.59 feet

6. Which ordered pair represents the solution to the following linear system?

$$y = 3x - 7$$
$$y = -x + 5$$

  A. $(3, 2)$ **C.** $(2, 3)$

  B. $(-3, -2)$ **D.** $(2, -3)$

SAMPLE TEST A CONTINUED

7. Which of the following linear systems has the solution (1, 4)?

A. $y = 3x - 6$
$y = 5x + 5$

B. $y = 2x - 4$
$7y - x = 6$

C. $y = 3x + 1$
$2y - 5x = 3$

D. $5y = 12x - 4$
$2y - x = 5$

8. Which of the following is true?

A. A quadratic equation can always be solved using the quadratic formula.

B. Given 2 roots, I cannot always write the quadratic equation.

C. The term x^2 will have a negative coefficient if the parabola opens down.

D. All of the above

9. Determine the area of the figure.

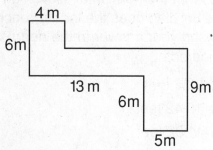

A. 102

B. 114

C. 124

D. 144

10. A rectangular piece of cloth 15 centimeters long is cut along a diagonal to form two triangles. One of the triangles has a side length of 9 centimeters. Which is a true statement?

A. The second triangle has an angle measure of 15° by CPCTC.

B. The second triangle has a side length of 9 centimeters by CPCTC.

C. The second triangle has a side length of 18 cm by CPCTC.

D. You cannot make a conclusion about the side length of the second triangle.

11. Which is the best estimate of the length of each side of a square that has an area of 80 cm^2?

12. Which number has the greatest absolute value?

A. $-\sqrt{81}$

B. -10.2

C. $-\dfrac{360}{12}$

D. -9.75

MN Test Prep Grade 9

SAMPLE TEST A CONTINUED

13. What is the volume of a sphere with a radius of 4.5 feet?

$\left(\text{Hint: } V = \dfrac{4\pi r^3}{3}\right)$

A. 254.47 cubic feet

B. 381.70 cubic feet

C. 563.23 cubic feet

D. 1,145.45 cubic feet

14. What is the distance between points (1, 5) and (−8, 4). Round to the nearest hundredth.

A. 6.06

B. 9.06

C. 7.5

D. 10.06

15. Let b be the base of an exponential function. Which represents all the restrictions on b?

A. $b \geq 0$

B. $b < 0$

C. $b \leq 0$

D. $b \neq 0$

16. Which power of 5 is closest to 11^8?

A. 5^{11}

B. 5^{12}

C. 5^{13}

D. 5^{14}

17. The Davis family's monthly budget is as follows:

Mortgage	1200
Food	1000
Clothing	400
Savings	300
Other	100
Total	$3000

Which would be the best display of data to use?

A. Line graph

B. Bar graph

C. Circle graph

D. Pictograph

18. If the speed of light is 3.00×10^8 meters per second, how far would a beam of light travel in 7,500 seconds?

A. 2.00×10^8

B. 2.25×10^8

C. 2.25×10^{11}

D. 2.25×10^{12}

19. Maria is a plumber. The amount she charges is based on the number of hours that she works. The total charge in dollars, T, is given as a function of the number of hours, h, by the equation $T = 75h + 60$. Which sentence best describes her charges?

A. She charges $60 per hour.

B. She charges $60 for the first hour and $75 for each additional hour.

C. She charges $75 per hour plus a house call fee of $60.

D. She charges $60 per hour plus a house call fee of $75.

20. Using the graph, find the difference between the greatest amount of money raised and the least amount of money raised.

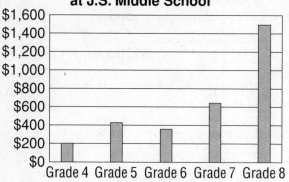

Amount of Fundraising at J.S. Middle School

A. $1,000   **C.** $1,300

B. $1,200   **D.** $1,400

21. Marianne is doing a word problem that says the sum of three consecutive even numbers is 42. The equation that she sets up is $n + (n + 2) + (n + 4) = 42$. What does the variable n represent?

A. The smallest of the three numbers

B. The average of the number

C. The middle number

D. None of the above

22. Write the equation of the line perpendicular to the one below and with the same y-intercept as the one below.

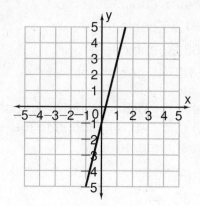

A. $y = -\frac{1}{4}x + 1$

B. $y = \frac{1}{4}x - 1$

C. $y = \frac{1}{4}x + 1$

D. $y = -\frac{1}{4}x - 1$

23. Which of the following is the correct translation of 9 less than p is greater than or equal to 30?

A. $p + 9 \le 30$

B. $9 + p \ge 30$

C. $p - 9 \ge 30$

D. $9 - p \le 30$

SAMPLE TEST A CONTINUED

24. Which of these is a diagonal of pentagon *ABCEH*?

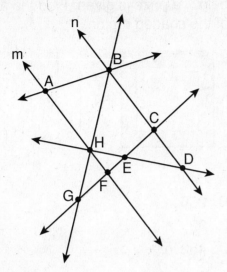

A. $\overline{BH}$ **C.** $\overline{EH}$

B. $\overline{FC}$ **D.** $\overline{BC}$

25. Which placement of the parentheses makes the statement true?

    A. $8(20 - 8) + 11^2 = 228$

    B. $8 \times 20 - (8 + 11^2) = 228$

    C. $(8 \times 20 - 8) + 11^2 = 228$

    D. None of the above

26. Solve the inequality for *x*.

    $4x \geq -32x - 3$

    A. $x \geq -12$

    B. $x \geq -\dfrac{1}{12}$

    C. $x \leq \dfrac{1}{12}$

    D. $x \leq 12$

27. The ordered pairs shown form a quadratic pattern.

x	y
0	−3
1	−2
2	1
3	6
4	13
5	??

What is the missing *y*-value?

    A. 20

    B. 21

    C. 22

    D. 23

28. If $ABC \cong FED$, write a proportion you can use to find the measure of $\overline{BC}$.

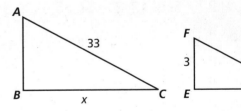

    A. $\dfrac{3}{x} = \dfrac{33}{5}$

    B. $3(33) = 5x$

    C. $3x = 5(33)$

    D. $\dfrac{5}{33} = \dfrac{3}{x}$

SAMPLE TEST A CONTINUED

29. A solid has 4 congruent triangular faces and 1 square face. What is the solid?

   A. Triangular pyramid

   B. Rectangular pyramid

   C. Square pyramid

   D. Rectangular prism

30. What is the equation of the line that is perpendicular to $y = -2x + 7$ and passes through the point $(-9, -8)$?

   A. $y = \frac{1}{2}x - \frac{5}{2}$

   B. $y = 2x - 5$

   C. $y = \frac{1}{2}x - \frac{7}{2}$

   D. $y = -\frac{1}{2}x - \frac{7}{2}$

31. Find the mean of the data below.

   1, 1, 2, 3, 5, 8, 13, 21, 34, 55

   A. About 12

   B. About 14

   C. About 16

   D. About 18

32. Identify the transformation.

   A. Glide reflection

   B. Dilation

   C. Translation

   D. Rotation

33. If a beanbag is tossed and lands in the shaded area of the square shown below, a prize is given. Find the area of the shaded region.

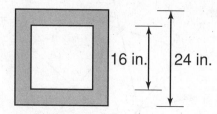

   A. 64 in.^{2}

   B. 256 in.^{2}

   C. 320 in.^{2}

   D. 452 in.^{2}

34. Which part in the quadratic equation is the discriminant?

   A. $-b$

   B. $b^2 - 4ac$

   C. $2a$

   D. $\sqrt{b^2 - 4ac}$

35. Which value is equivalent to $\frac{4^{-25}}{4^{-12}}$?

   A. 4^{-37}

   B. 4^{-13}

   C. 4^{12}

   D. 4^{13}

MN Test Prep Grade 9

36. A car uses 20 gallons of gas during a 450 mile trip. How far can the driver go if there are 7 gallons of gasoline in the tank? Round your answer to the nearest whole mile.

    A. 57.5 mi

    B. 157.5 mi

    C. 257.5 mi

    D. 357.5 mi

37. Which value of z is a solution to $5z - z = 2 + 10$?

    A. -3

    B. 3

    C. 4

    D. 12

38. Max's school has a rectangular courtyard that measures 96 meters by 72 meters. How much shorter is the walk from the library to the school along the diagonal sidewalk than through point A?

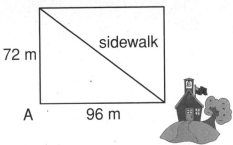

    A. 48 m   **C.** 96 m

    B. 88 m   **D.** 120 m

39. A and B are on the edges of a ravine. What is AB?

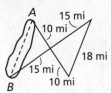

    A. 48 m   **C.** 96 m

    B. 88 m   **D.** 120 m

40. Thomas is a quality control inspector. He examined 113 cabinet doors in one hour. He found 9 of them to be defective. He anticipates that he will inspect 745 doors during the remaining 7 hours of his shift. Which proportion models cabinet doors inspected to defective doors found in the first hour compared to the remainder of the shift?

    A. $\dfrac{x}{7 \text{ hours}} = \dfrac{113 \text{ doors}}{1 \text{ hour}}$

    B. $\dfrac{x}{745 \text{ doors}} = \dfrac{113 \text{ doors}}{7 \text{ hours}}$

    C. $\dfrac{745 \text{ doors}}{113 \text{ doors}} = \dfrac{9 \text{ defective}}{x}$

    D. $\dfrac{113 \text{ doors}}{9 \text{ defective}} = \dfrac{745 \text{ doors}}{x}$

SAMPLE TEST A CONTINUED

41. What is (are) the root(s) of the quadratic equation $y = x^2 + 4x + 4$?

A. 2

B. 5 and 6

C. −2

D. 2 and −2

42. The perimeter of the Jacobsens' yard is 750 feet. What is the length of s?

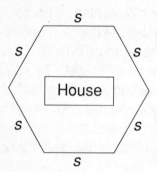

A. 110 feet **C.** 125 feet

B. 120 feet **D.** 130 feet

43. A coin is flipped twice in a row. What is the probability of getting two heads?

A. $\frac{1}{2}$

B. $\frac{1}{3}$

C. $\frac{1}{4}$

D. $\frac{1}{5}$

44. City planners want to make a building lot out of a piece of land that is 150 ft more than its width. It is to have the same proportions as a city lot that is 250 feet wide and 300 feet long. What is the smallest dimension of the new lot? Round your answer to the nearest whole foot.

A. 300 feet **C.** 750 feet

B. 500 feet **D.** 975 feet

45. Lisa bought a new sewing machine on a financial installment plan. She made a down payment of $100 and has to make 18 monthly payments of $75 each. How much money would she have saved if she had paid $1160 in cash?

A. $1,450.00

B. $1,160.00

C. $190.00

D. $290.00

46. Find the measure of the missing side of the following right triangle to the nearest hundredth.

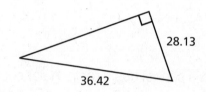

A. 13.23

B. 22.13

C. 23.13

D. 83.23

SAMPLE TEST A CONTINUED

47. Mitchell is paid twice the normal hourly wage for each hour he works over 40 hours in a week. Last week he worked 50 hours and earned $754.20. What is Mitchell's hourly wage?

   A. $11.72

   B. $12.57

   C. $13.55

   D. $18.86

48. Kate and Ben are planning a surprise party for their parents' anniversary. They estimate that 50 people will attend. The caterer suggests they order 2 sandwiches per person and 25 extra sandwiches. How many sandwiches should they order?

   A. 75

   B. 100

   C. 125

   D. 175

49. Which statement is FALSE?

   A. In a 45°-45°-90° triangle, all sides are equal in length.

   B. In a 45°-45°-90° triangle, all sides are of different length.

   C. In a 45°-45°-90° triangle, each leg is equal to the length of the hypotenuse times $\sqrt{2}$.

   D. All of the above

50. On Mothers Day, 2005, the United States Census Bureau estimated there were approximately 62.5 million women in the United States who were mothers. If each mother received one $2.00 greeting card, approximately how much money would the greeting card industry earn on Mother's Day?

   A. 1.25×10^8

   B. 6.25×10^7

   C. 3.15×10^7

   D. 1.25×10^6

51. If the length of a rectangle were doubled, the area of the rectangle would increase by:

   A. 1.5 times

   B. 2 times

   C. 3 times

   D. 4 times

52. From which three-dimensional figure can you obtain a circular cross-section?

   A. Cube

   B. Pyramid

   C. Cone

   D. Triangular prism

SAMPLE TEST A CONTINUED

53. From looking at the table, which equation best describes the relationship between the number of students and the number of tables in the cafeteria?

Number of students (*n*)	Number of tables in cafeteria (*t*)
720	18
600	15
960	24

A. $t = 40n$

B. $n = 40t$

C. $n = 35t + 90$

D. $t = 35n + 90$

54. Which inequality represents the phrase "3 is less than a number increased by 4 and then multiplied by −2"?

A. $3 > x + (4)(-2)$

B. $3 < x + (4)(-2)$

C. $-2(x + 4) > 3$

D. $-2(x + 4) < 3$

Gridded-Response: Fill in the grid with your answer to each question.

55. Find the mode of the data below.

1, 1, 2, 3, 5, 8, 13, 21, 34, 55

56. The ratio of the corresponding sides of 2 similar triangles is 2 : 6. The sides of the larger triangle are 12 yards, 15 yards, and 18 yards. What is the perimeter of the smaller triangle?

Extended-Response: Show your work.

57. The graph shows the average attendance at football games at Big University. What are the mean, mode, median, and range of the attendance? Which statistic best reflects the central tendency of the attendance data?

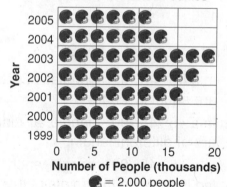

Attendance at Football Games

= 2,000 people

Name_____ Date _____ Class_____

PRACTICE TEST B

Select the best answer for each question.

Use the graph to answer questions 1 and 2.

The graph gives the value of Kristine's color copier since she purchased it.

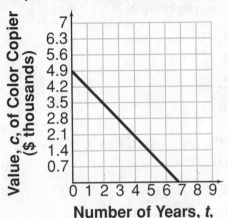

Number of Years, *t*, Since Purchase

1. What is the equation of the line?

   A. $c = -7t + 490$

   B. $c = -0.7t + 4.9$

   C. $c = 0.7t + 49$

   D. $c = -7t + 49$

2. How much was the copier worth 4 years after Kristine purchased it?

   A. $1,800

   B. $2,100

   C. $2,400

   D. $3,000

3. A movie store has two membership plans. Plan A is a monthly fee of $15, and a $2 per movie rented. Plan B is a monthly fee of $30, and $1 per movie rented. How many movies would you have to rent for Plan B to be clearly better than Plan A?

   A. 10

   B. 14

   C. 16

   D. 29

4. The sun has an angle of elevation of 42° Katherine is 64 inches tall. How long is her shadow?

   A. 42.82 in.

   B. 47.56 in.

   C. 57.63 in.

   D. 71.08 in.

5. When the expression $1 + \sqrt{4}$ is simplified, which is the result?

   A. $1 - 2i$

   B. $1 + 2i$

   C. 3

   D. -1

PRACTICE TEST B CONTINUED

6. Solve the following inequality:

$$-4(x + 3) > 16$$

A. $x > 7$

B. $x < 7$

C. $x > -7$

D. $x < -7$

7. Point A (2, −3) is translated to the left 3 units and up 4 units. What are the coordinates of A'?

A. (−1, 1)

B. (0, 0)

C. (5, −7)

D. (−1, 7)

8. Which is NOT a part of the intersection of the two sets?

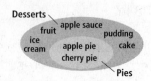

A. Cake

B. Fruit

C. Ice cream

D. All of the above

9. Describe the solution of $4x \leq 16$.

A. All real numbers less than 4

B. All real numbers less than or equal to 4

C. All real numbers greater than or equal to 4

D. All real numbers less than 16

10. Evaluate $x^5 - 23x^2 + 45x - 34$ for $x = 2$.

A. −10

C. −4

B. −6

D. 0

11. How many faces does a pentagonal pyramid have?

A. 3

B. 4

C. 5

D. 6

12. Which equation has a solution of $x = 3$?

A. $3x - 2 = 4$

B. $6x - 2 = 16$

C. $10 - 3x = -1$

D. $-2 - 5x = -13$

13. Find the median of the data below.

1, 1, 2, 3, 5, 8, 13, 21, 34, 55

A. 1

B. 5

C. 6.5

D. 8

PRACTICE TEST B CONTINUED

14. A manufacturer ships coffee mugs in boxes that measure 4 inches × 4 inches × 3.5 inches. If he packages as many boxes with mugs as possible inside a shipping box that measures 18 inches × 18 inches × 20 inches, how much space is left inside for packaging material?

   A. 880 cubic inches

   B. 6,424 cubic inches

   C. 6,480 cubic inches

   D. 7,280 cubic inches

15. Rewrite 4^{-2} without an exponent.

   A. 16

   B. −16

   C. $\dfrac{1}{16}$

   D. $-\dfrac{1}{16}$

16. Which statement is true?

   A. In a 30°-60°-90° triangle, the length of the hypotenuse is $\sqrt{3}$ times the length of the shorter leg.

   B. In a 30°-60°-90° triangle, the length of the hypotenuse is $2\sqrt{3}$ times the length of the longer leg.

   C. In a 30°-60°-90° triangle, the length of the hypotenuse is $2\sqrt{3}$ times the length of the shorter leg.

   D. None of the above

17. Bench's Greenhouse sells foil-wrapped poinsettias. They have 3100 poinsettias in the green house with 1700 that need to be wrapped. Foil wrap is packaged 50 wraps per box. How many boxes of wrap are needed?

   A. 34

   B. 50

   C. 62

   D. 170

18. What is the domain of the following function?

$$y = \sqrt{x}$$

   A. All positive real numbers and 0

   B. All negative real numbers and 0

   C. All real numbers

   D. All Integers

19. How long is the side of a square if its diagonal is 85 inches? Find the answer to the nearest inch.

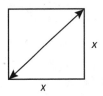

   A. 170 inches   **C.** 210 inches

   B. 7,225 inches   **D.** 60 inches

     MN Test Prep Grade 9

PRACTICE TEST B CONTINUED

20. Mrs. Podach saved $455 for a new washing machine. She plans to save an additional $15 per week. In how many weeks will she have enough to buy a washing machine that costs $699, NOT including tax?

A. 15

B. 17

C. 25

D. 244

21. The height and base of the outside right triangle below measure 28 ft and 18 ft respectively. A vertical line is drawn from the hypotenuse to the base two feet from the left edge. How high will it be? Round your answer to the nearest hundredth of a foot.

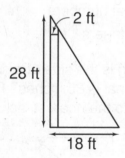

A. 23.11 ft

B. 24.00 ft

C. 24.89 ft

D. 25.32 ft

22. A standard six-sided die is rolled. What is the probability of getting an even number less than 3?

A. $\frac{1}{3}$

B. $\frac{1}{4}$

C. $\frac{1}{5}$

D. $\frac{1}{6}$

23. What is the circumference of a circle with radius 8 inches? Use $\pi = 3.14$.

A. 25.12 inches

B. 50.24 inches

C. 100.48 inches

D. 200.96 inches

24. Katy likes to catch butterflies. The equation $b = -2(x - 3)^2 + 10$ models this hobby, where b is the number of butterflies caught for the hour and x is the number of hours after she started catching. She will catch the maximum amount per hour after _____ hours.

A. 10 hours

B. 3 hours

C. 4 hours

D. 5 hours

 MN Test Prep Grade 9

PRACTICE TEST B CONTINUED

25. Thomas is a quality control inspector. He examined 113 cabinet doors in one hour. He found 9 of them to be defective. He anticipates that he will inspect 745 doors during the remaining 7 hours of his shift. How many defective cabinet doors can Thomas expect to find during the whole shift?

   A. 9

   B. 50

   C. 59

   D. 69

26. Which shows a pairs of equivalent numbers?

   A. $|-6|$ and 6

   B. $|6|$ and 6

   C. $|-6|$ and -6

   D. A and B are correct.

27. A 20-ft ladder is placed 4 feet from a building and leaned against the building. How high up the building does the ladder reach? Round to the nearest tenth of a foot.

   A. 16.0 feet

   B. 20.4 feet

   C. 13.7 feet

   D. 19.6 feet

28. Which value of s is the solution to this equation?

$$34 + 2s = -56 - 3s$$

   A. -20

   B. -18

   C. 18

   D. 20

29. Hector has 6 times as many coins as Wilma. If Hector has 126 coins, which equation would you use to find out how many coins Wilma has?

   A. $c + 6 = 126$

   B. $6c = 126$

   C. $c = \dfrac{126 + 6}{6}$

   D. $126c = 6$

30. Which operation should be performed first to simplify the following expression?

$$-24\left(18 - 2^2\right) \div 14$$

   A. Subtraction

   B. Multiplication

   C. Division

   D. Squaring

31. Which ordered pair represents the solution to the following linear system?

$$y + 3x = 12$$
$$4y + 3x = 30?$$

A. (2, 6)

B. (−2, −6)

C. (6, 2)

D. (6, −2)

32. Triangle *ABC* is similar to triangle *DEA* Find the measure of angle *x*.

A. 32°

B. 51°

C. 64°

D. 116°

33. This figure appears to be symmetric with respect to

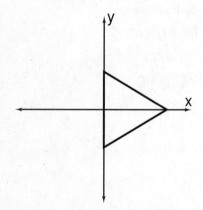

A. The *x*-axis

B. The *y*-axis

C. Both the *x*-axis and *y*-axis

D. Neither the *x*- nor the *y*-axis

34. A local hockey player has scored the following number of goals in the past 9 games:

1, 2, 0, 1, 2, 1, 1, 3, 2

How many goals must he score in the next 6 games in order to average 2 goals per game for the season?

A. 7   **C.** 17

B. 12   **D.** 30

35. One ad claims that 8 out of 10 households in your neighborhood use XYZ sink cleaner. If your neighborhood has 65 houses, how many of them use XYZ?

A. 8

B. 10

C. 52

D. 65

36. A triangle has angles 35°, 55° and 90°. The hypotenuse is 10 cm long. What is the length of the shortest side to the nearest tenth of a centimeter?

A. 5.7 cm

B. 8.2 cm

C. 7.0 cm

D. 9.2 cm

PRACTICE TEST B CONTINUED

37. A model builder wants to model a right triangular lot that has legs of 135 feet and 75 feet. The model is to have its longer leg 4 inches longer than the shorter leg. Find the dimensions of the shorter leg.

   A. 3 in.

   B. 5 in.

   C. 7 in.

   D. 11 in.

38. You are in charge of buying bags of pretzels and popcorn for the school picnic. A bag of pretzels costs $3.00 and a bag of popcorn costs $4. You have $48 to spend. What does m represent in the table?

Popcorn	Pretzels
0	16
3	12
6	8
9	m
12	0

   A. 0   **C.** 4

   B. 2   **D.** 6

39. Which type of transformation is shown below?

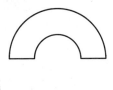

   A. translation

   B. rotation

   C. reflection

   D. glide reflection

40. Use the order of operations to simplify.

$$2^3 - 7 + 16 \div (-3 + 5)$$

   A. $8\frac{1}{2}$

   B. $-2\frac{1}{8}$

   C. 3

   D. 9

41. Which figure is NOT a quadrilateral?

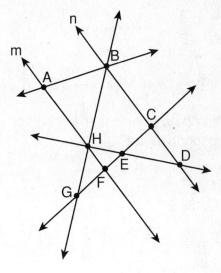

   A. *ABDH*

   B. *BCDH*

   C. *BCEH*

   D. *BCFH*

42. Margot walks her neighbor's dog every 3rd day. Her friend Karen walks her neighbor's dog every 7th day. They meet each other on the sidewalk on July 1st. On what date will they next meet?

   A. July 3rd

   B. July 15th

   C. July 21st

   D. August 1st

MN Test Prep Grade 9

PRACTICE TEST B CONTINUED

43. Find the coordinates of the point on $\overline{AB}$ that is one-fourth the distance from A to B for $A(10, -1)$ and $B(12, -9)$.

A. (11.5, -3)

B. (11, -3)

C. (10.5, -3)

D. (10.5, -5)

44. What is the *y*-intercept for $5x = y + 7$?

A. -7

B. -2

C. 7

D. 12

45. Which number has the greatest absolute value?

A. $\dfrac{-120}{2}$

B. -59.9

C. $\dfrac{206}{4}$

D. 59.75

46. Which of the following angle values would disprove a triangle conjecture?

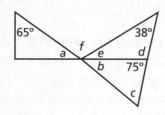

A. $d = 135$

B. $a = 18$

C. $d = 125$

D. $e = 31$

47. What is the approximate volume in cubic inches of a cylinder with a radius of 4 inches and a height of 12 inches? (Use 3.14 for π)

A. 150.72

B. 301.44

C. 602.88

D. 1,205.76

48. Which would be a possible set of intervals for a histogram of this set of data?

```
99 55 78 91 30 82 88 92 69
35 79 70 82 45 38 54 92 87
80 34 40 20 87 92 94 48 73
```

A. 10 to 29, 30 to 49, 50 to 79

B. 20 to 49, 50 to 79, 80 to 109

C. 20 to 29, 30 to 39, 40 to 49, 50 to 59, 60 to 69, 70 to 79, 80 to 89, 90 to 100

D. 40 to 49, 50 to 59, 60 to 69, 70 to 79, 80 to 89, 90 to 100

49. Evaluate $\left(\dfrac{7}{3}\right)^{-3}$.

A. $\dfrac{343}{9}$

B. $\dfrac{49}{9}$

C. $\dfrac{27}{343}$

D. $\dfrac{49}{27}$

MN Test Prep Grade 9

50. Which expression is equivalent to 4^{x-4x}?

A. $\dfrac{4^x}{4^{4x}}$

B. $\dfrac{4^x}{4^{-4x}}$

C. $\dfrac{4}{4^{x-4x}}$

D. $\dfrac{1}{4^{x+4x}}$

51. The coordinates of the endpoints of a diameter of a circle are (4, 7) and (−6, 3). Find the coordinates of the center.

A. (−1, 5)   C. (−1, 6)

B. (0, 5)   D. (0, 6)

52. Regita collected data on the kinds of sandwiches her customers want at her deli shop. The table shows her findings.

Sandwich	Number of Customers
Ham	26
Turkey	25
Chicken	15
Roast Beef	22
Corned Beef	12

Assuming that a similar trend in sandwich preferences continues, what is the probability that the next customer will order a ham sandwich?

A. $\dfrac{1}{100}$ C. $\dfrac{13}{50}$

B. $\dfrac{21}{100}$ D. $\dfrac{67}{100}$

53. Which value of h makes the inequality true?

$\dfrac{3}{4}(24 + 8h) > 2(5h + 1)$

A. $h < 2\dfrac{3}{4}$

B. $h < 4$

C. $h > \dfrac{17}{4}$

D. $h > 5$

54. The table shows the total dollar amount of ticket sales for two very popular movies.

Movie	Total Sales
Titanic	$600,788,000
Jurassic Park	$357,067,000

Which is the best estimate of how many times greater the ticket sales for *Titanic* were than for *Jurassic Park*?

A. $\dfrac{2}{3}$ times as great

B. $1\dfrac{1}{2}$ times as great

C. $2\dfrac{2}{3}$ times as great

D. 3 times as great

55. A swimming pool charges a $75 membership fee per year and $1.50 each time you bring a guest. Which equation shows the yearly cost y in terms of the number of guests g?

A. $y = 75g + 1.5$

B. $y = -1.5g + 75$

C. $y = 1.5g + 75$

D. $y = 1.5g + 75g$

PRACTICE TEST B CONTINUED

56. For the equation $y = 3x^2$, what does x equal if $y = 27$?

   A. −3, −4

   B. 0, 6.54

   C. −0.46, −6.54

   D. 3, −3

57. What is the midpoint of $(−8, −4)$ and $(14, 8)$?

   A. $(−3, −2)$ **C.** $(−11, −6)$

   B. $(3, 2)$ **D.** $(11, 6)$

58. Which number sentence is false?

   A. $0 > −17$

   B. $−56 < −47$

   C. $32 > 2$

   D. $−88 > 0$

59. Which statement is FALSE about any tangent of a circle?

   A. A tangent is perpendicular to a radius at the point that it intersects the circle.

   B. A tangent intersects a circle at exactly one point.

   C. A tangent may go through the center of the circle.

   D. Tangents drawn from a point outside the circle are equal in length.

60. A swimming pool charges a $75 membership fee per year, and $1.50 each time you bring a guest. Which expression shows the yearly cost y in terms of the number of guests g?

   A. $75g + 1.5$

   B. $−1.5g + 75$

   C. $1.5g + 75$

   D. $1.5g + 75g$

Gridded-Response: Fill in the grid with your answer to each question.

61. What is another way to write 3^4?

62. A 15-pound bag of onions sells for $18.75. At this rate, how much will a ten pound bag cost? Round your answer to the nearest cent.

Extended-Response: Show your work for each question.

63. The table shows a linear relationship between x and y.

x	y
−2	3
0	7
2	11
4	15
6	??

   A. Explain how you would find the missing value in the table.

   B. Graph the function represented by the table. Write the equation of the line and identify the slope and y-intercept.

64. Consider the inequality $2x + 8 < 3x + 4$.

   A. Solve the inequality and graph the solution on a number line. Write out the steps in your solution and justify each step.

   B. How is the solution set of the inequality related to the solution of the equation $2x + 8 = 3x + 4$?

          MN Test Prep Grade 9